Instructor's Resource Manual with Test Items to Accompany:

Working in Groups
Communication Principles and Strategies

Third Edition

Prepared by:
Patricia Ganer
Cypress College

Isa Engleberg
Prince George's Community College

Dianna Wynn
Courtroom Intelligence

Houghton Mifflin Company Boston New York

Sponsoring Editor: Adam Forrand
Editorial Associate: Brigitte Maser
Associate Editor: Kristen Desmond LeFevre
Project Editor: Claudine Bellanton
Manufacturing Coordinator: Jane Spelman
Marketing Manager: Barbara LeBuhn

Printed in the U.S.A.

ISBN: 0-618-21567-0

123456789—VG—06 05 04 03 02

TABLE OF CONTENTS

INTRODUCTION: PREPARING TO TEACH THE COURSE ***1***

Using the Instructor's Resource Manual 2
Sample Course Syllabus 4
Sixteen Week Course Outline 6
Ten Week Course Outline 7
Group Communication Library 8

ASSESSMENT OPTIONS FOR GRADED ASSIGNMENTS ***13***

Problem-Solving Discussion 14
Group Presentation Project 16
Real World Group Presentation 18
Group Analysis Paper 20
Twelve Angry Men Analysis Paper 21
Groupwork Log 22
Decision-Making Competencies 23
Participation Assessment Instrument 24
Post- Meeting Reaction (PMR) Form 25
Oral Presentation Scale 26

GROUPWORK: ACTIVITIES FOR WORKING IN GROUPS ***27***

Initial Class Meetings 28
Autograph Hunt 29
Why Are You Taking This Course? 30
Getting Acquainted 32
The Dinner Party 34

Chapter 1: Introduction to Small Group Communication ***35***

It Was the Best of Groups; It Was the Worst of Groups 35
Speak Your Mind About College 37
How Big is Small? 39
Pieces of a Puzzle 41

Chapter 2: Group Formation and Development ***43***

Classroom Norms 43
Meeting Needs 44
Unfulfilled FIRO Needs 45
Group Expectations 47

Chapter 3: Participation in Groups ***49***

Type Talk in Groups 49
Functional Role Playing 51
The Best Group for the Job 54
Myers-Briggs Types: Vive La Difference 56
Talking Tokens 57

Chapter 4: Confidence in Groups ***59***
Sorting the Symptoms 59
Cognitive Restructuring 60
Systematic Desensitization 62
I Don't Mean to Brag But 64
Chapter 5: Verbal and Nonverbal Communication in Groups ***65***
Context, Context, Context 65
Space Invasion 66
How Often is Often 67
Please Be Seated 69
One Syllable Talk: An Intercultural Experience 70
Name That Emotion 71
Teacher, You Made a Mistake 72
Everyone Knows What I Mean 73
Chapter 6: Listening in Groups ***75***
Hold Your Tongue and Listen 75
Four Squares 76
Are You Listening 79
Listening Triads 80
Different Notes for Different Folks 81
Listening Excuses, Excuses, Excuses 82
Listening to Learn 83
Chapter 7: Conflict and Cohesion in Groups ***85***
Win as Much as You Can 85
Meet the Mediator 88
What's in a Name? 90
They Never Ask for Directions 91
You Too? 92
Please Don't Say That 94
Chapter 8: Leadership in Groups ***95***
Wanted: A Few Good Leaders 95
Natural Born Leaders 96
Select a Leader 97
Battle of the Sexes 100
What Constitutes Effective Leadership? 101
Extraordinary Leaders 103
They Drove Me Crazy 104
Chapter 9: Decision Making and Problem Solving in Groups ***105***
Game Building 105
Lost on the Moon 106
Ozone Collapse Scenario 110
Planning with PERT 113
Selling the Brooklyn Bridge 114
So That's What it Means 115
One Step at a Time 118

Chapter 10: Argumentation in Groups ***121***
Divide and Debate 121
Group Debate 122
Class Code of Ethics 123
Red Rover, Red Rover 124
Chapter 11: Motivating Groups ***125***
Your Guiding Motive 125
It Was the Best of Teams 128
Time Out to Celebrate! 129
Candygram 130
Chapter 12: Informed Groups ***131***
Research Scavenger Hunt 131
A Meeting of Minds 133
Name That Source 134
Do as I Say 136
Chapter 13: Technology and Virtual Groups ***139***
Computer and Teleconference Simulation 139
I Want to be a Telecommuter 141
Techs and the Campus 142
Chapter 14: Planning and Conducting Meetings ***143***
Meet the People Problems 143
We Have to Stop Meeting Like This 145
Planning a Meeting 146
Creating an Agenda 147
What Do the Minutes Reveal? 149
Designing an Agenda Form 150
Chapter 15: Making Presentations in Groups ***151***
A Practice Speech 151
Common Ground 153
Choosing Visual Aids 154
Show Me the Slides 155
Appendix: Parliamentary Procedure ***157***
The Mascot Debate 157
I Move That 158
Government in Action 159
Hear, Hear 160
Who Wants to be a Parliamentarian? 161

TESTBANK	***163***
Chapter 1	164
Chapter 2	169
Chapter 3	174
Chapter 4	180
Chapter 5	185
Chapter 6	190
Chapter 7	195
Chapter 8	200
Chapter 9	205
Chapter 10	211
Chapter 11	216
Chapter 12	221
Chapter 13	226
Chapter 14	231
Chapter 15	236
Appendix	241

Introduction: Preparing to Teach the Course

USING THE INSTRUCTOR'S RESOURCE MANUAL

SAMPLE COURSE SYLLABUS

The sample syllabus in this manual provides a blueprint to help you prepare to teach the small group communication course. After inserting specific course and instructor information, the syllabus is ready to distribute to students with little or no modification. Experienced instructors will find the syllabus easy to modify to suit their instructional approaches.

The syllabus includes course outcomes linked to each chapter of the textbook. Basic course policies can be modified to reflect individual preferences for conducting a class. However, we strongly recommend that a clear attendance policy be established for a group communication course. The frequent use of exercises requires a student's presence in order to fully internalize the material. The grading procedure reflects our belief that at least half of a student's final grade should be based on his or her performance in groups.

Two course outlines have been provided. The first one is designed for a sixteen-week semester; the second outline follows a ten-week format. The outlines specify the discussion topics and accompanying chapter readings for each week. In the Groupwork and Assessment sections, we have identified the activities in the student's text. The Instructor's Resource Manual offers several more exercises in each section. You may modify the sequence of assigned chapters or choose from other Groupwork activities provided in the textbook or in the Instructor's Resource Manual.

INSTRUCTOR'S LIBRARY

Many publications have informed our teaching and the development of this textbook. We have provided a list of both trade press books and academic publications that have been particularly useful. You may want to consider selections from this list as you expand your personal library or request materials for your college library.

GRADED ASSIGNMENTS

Options for graded student assignments are included in this manual. The assignments are ready to be reproduced or can be modified before distribution to your class. The two major group assignments include explanations of the assignment requirements and the grading criteria. The sample syllabus requires students to complete both the Problem-Solving Discussion and the Group Presentation Project.

Two options for group analysis papers are provided. The first option requires students to analyze the behavior of a group in which they are working on a class project. This paper should be assigned in conjunction with one or both of the graded group assignments. The second option requires students to analyze the group interaction represented in the film *Twelve Angry Men.* This film is usually available from major video retail outlets. In addition to the analysis papers, a Groupwork log assignment is included. The log is a flexible assignment. Students could be required to describe and analyze the behavior and progress of an ongoing group or comment on in-class group activities.

Each chapter of the textbook includes an assessment instrument. These instruments can be used as grading forms, for peer evaluation, or for self-assessment.

GROUPWORK

The Instructor's Resource Manual includes many options for in-class activities linked to the concepts discussed in each chapter of the textbook. All Groupwork activities that appear in the textbook are also available in the Instructor's Resource Manual with more detailed explanations. It will not be possible to use all the exercises during the semester. We have attempted to provide a variety of approaches in each section. Instructors work differently with material; you may wish to experiment until you find the exercises that work best for you. "Get-Acquainted" activities appropriate for the beginning of the term are also included.

Each Groupwork activity identifies the goal(s) of the activity and the number of participants. Detailed instructions are provided to aid the instructor in facilitating the activity in the classroom. Most of the activities are followed by teaching tips, which include discussion questions. The debriefing process is critical as these questions can help students process what they have learned from the group experience.

TEST BANK

The test bank provides textbook-based examination questions for each chapter. A variety of testing formats are represented: multiple choice items, true/false statements, and essay questions. You can select from among the items provided for each chapter to develop texts or quizzes. Most instructors will cover several chapters per test. The sample syllabus suggests a total of three tests.

TEACHING AIDS

Available on-line for your convenience at http://college.hmco.com/communication are Power Point Slides that can be downloaded and repurposed as you see fit along with the entire Instructor Resource Manual with Test Items. Self-tests are also available for the student to test their knowledge of the material in each chapter and to better prepare them for class and learning about small group communication.

We hope that *Working in Groups* and the accompanying Instructor's Resource Manual effectively serve your needs and those of your students. If you have questions, comments, or suggestions for improving the textbook, please feel free to contact us.

Isa Engleberg
Prince George's Community College
Speech Communication & Theatre Department
301 Largo Road
Largo, Maryland 20744-2199
Email: iengleberg@pgcc.edu.

Dianna Wynn
Courtroom Intelligence
1921 Polenta Road
Clayton, NC 27520
Email: drwynn@earthlink.net

SAMPLE COURSE SYLLABUS

Course Number and Title
Course Section Number
Course Meeting Time
Classroom Location

INSTRUCTOR:

PHONE:

EMAIL ADDRESS:

OFFICE:

OFFICE HOURS:

TEXTBOOK

Engleberg, Isa N., and Wynn, Dianna R. (2003). Working in Groups: Communication Principles and Strategies (3rd ed.). Boston, MA: Houghton Mifflin.

COURSE OUTCOMES

Upon completion of the course, students should be able to

- Understand the necessity of working effectively in a variety of groups
- Understand how groups develop and reflect personal and collective needs.
- Demonstrate effective leadership skills with an understanding of leadership theories and adaptive communication strategies.
- Participate effectively in a group with an understanding of theories and principles of participation.
- Manage their own communication apprehension and be supportive of less confident group members.
- Demonstrate effective listening behaviors within a group.
- Use language and nonverbal behavior to create a supportive group communication climate.
- Resolve group conflict and promote cohesion among members.
- Plan and participate in meetings, including the appropriate use of parliamentary procedure and the preparation of meeting agendas and minutes.
- Select and use appropriate decision-making and problem-solving procedures.
- Present sound arguments to a group and work with other members to prepare a group presentation.
- Assess a group's information needs and gather valid information from a variety of sources.
- Understand the nature of virtual groups and the factors affecting processes in group communication in the virtual environment.
- Understand and appreciate the influence of gender and cultural diversity on group interaction.
- Use strategies that effectively balance a variety of task and maintenance dimensions of small group communication.

COURSE POLICIES

- In a group communication course, your personal success and the success of the group depend upon everyone participating in the group activities. You are expected to attend class and actively participate in class discussions and activities. Your final grade will be lowered one full letter grade after three unexcused absences. Two late arrivals to class or early departures are equivalent to one absence.
- Attendance on group assignment days is mandatory. If you are absent, your group will complete the assignment without you and you will receive a 0 for the assignment. Time does not allow for group assignments to be made up. If an emergency does occur and you must be absent on the day of an assignment, call your instructor before class.
- You will take three written tests that will include material from the textbook, class discussions/lectures, and supplementary materials.
- In addition to in-class group activities, you will participate in two, graded group assignments. Class time will be provided to prepare for these assignments. However, you will be expected to meet with your group outside of class. Your grade for these assignments will be based on both your individual performance and the effectiveness of the entire group.
- When another group is scheduled to complete an assignment, you will be expected to observe the group and turn in an evaluation form. Poor listening behaviors during another group's presentation may result in a reduction in your group assignment grade.
- You will be required to turn in a group analysis paper, group agendas, and an individual bibliography. All written work should be typed. Excessive grammatical and typographical errors will result in a lower grade on the assignment.
- All written work should be turned in on the due date. Late work will result in a lowered grade.

GRADING PROCEDURE

Your grade for this course will be based on your performance on the following assignments. As you receive your grades, you should record them in the third column.

Assignment	Percentage	Grade
Problem-Solving Discussion	25%	
Group Presentation Project	25%	
Group Analysis Paper	15%	
Test 1	10%	
Test 2	10%	
Test 3	10%	
In-Class Activities	5%	

SIXTEEN WEEK COURSE OUTLINE

Week	Chapter	Topic	Groupwork	Assessment
1	1	Introduction to Small Group Communication	The Best of Groups	Basic Group Elements
2	2	Group Formation	Classroom Norms	Group Attraction Survey
3	3 4	Participation in Groups Confidence in Groups	Type Talk in Groups Sorting the Symptoms	Participation Assessment Instrument PRCA-24
4	5	Verbal and Nonverbal Communication	Context, Context, Context	Auditing Team Talk
5	6	Listening in Groups	Hold Your Tongue	Shafir's Test of Listening, Exam 1
6	7 8	Conflict and Cohesion Leadership in Groups	Win as Much as You Can, Wanted: A Few Good Leaders	Ross-DeWine, Least Preferred Co-worker
7	9	Decision Making and Problem Solving	Gamebuilding	Decision Making Competencies
8	10	Argumentation in Groups	Divide and Debate	Argumentativeness Scale
9		Problem-Solving Discussions		
10		Problem-Solving Discussions		
11	11	Motivating Groups	Your Guiding Motive	Team Motivation Inventory
12	12 13	Informed Groups Technology and Groups	Research Scavenger Hunt Computer and Telecommunication Simulation	Information Checklist Virtual Meeting Evaluation
13	15	Presentations in Groups	A Practice Speech	Oral Presentation Rating
14	14 Appendix	Planning and Conducting Meetings Parliamentary Procedure	Meet the People Problems The Mascot Debate	PMR Form Parliamentary Procedure Assessment
15		Group Presentation Projects		
16		Group Presentation Projects		

TEN WEEK COURSE OUTLINE

Week	Chapter	Topic	Groupwork	Assessment
1	1 2	Introduction to Small Group Communication Group Formation	The Best of Groups Classroom Norms	Basic Group Elements Group Attraction Survey
2	3 4	Participation in Groups Confidence in Groups	Type Talk in Groups Sorting the Symptoms	Participation Assessment Instrument PRCA-24
3	5 6	Verbal and Nonverbal Communication Listening in Groups	Context, Context, Context Hold Your Tongue	Audit Team Talk Shafir's Test of Listening, Exam 1
4	7 8	Conflict and Cohesion Leadership in Groups	Win as Much as You Can A Few Good Leaders	Ross-DeWine, Least Preferred Co-Worker
5	9 10	Decisions and Problems Argumentation in Groups	Game Building Divide and Debate	Decision Making Competencies Argumentativeness Scale
6		Problem-Solving Discussions		
7	11 12	Motivating Groups Informed Groups	Your Guiding Motive Research Scavenger Hunt	Team Motivation Inventory Information Checklist
8	13 15	Technology and Groups Making Presentations	Computer and Telecommunication Simulation A Practice Speech	Virtual Meeting Evaluation Oral Presentation Rating
9	14 Appendix	Planning and Conducting Meetings Parliamentary Procedure	Meet the People Problems The Mascot Debate	PMR Form Parliamentary Procedure Assessment
10		Group Presentation Projects		Exam 3

GROUP COMMUNICATION LIBRARY

The books on this resource list are sorted into general topics areas. A star (✱) indicates that we highly recommend this book for instructors. In many cases, the starred books can also serve as a recommended reading for students. Many of the listed books are trade books and can be found in major bookstores and through on-line booksellers.

This list does not contain journal articles or research summaries. Rather, it serves as a general reference library rather than a compilation of recent research. At the end of the list, we include the names of several communication/group research journals and relevant chapters from research handbooks.

Argumentation

Hollihan, T. A. & Baaske, K. T. (1994). *Arguments and arguing: The products and process of human decision making*. Prospect Heights, IL: Waveland.

Infante, D. A. (1988). *Arguing constructively*. Prospect Heights, IL: Waveland.

Kuhane, H. (1995). *Logic and contemporary rhetoric* (7th ed.). Belmont, CA: Wadsworth.

Lunsford, A. A. & Ruszkiewicz, J. J. (1999). *Everything's an argument*. Boston: Bedford/St. Martin's.

✱ Makau, J. M. & Marty, D. L. (2001). *Cooperative argumentation: A model for deliberative community*. Prospect Heights, IL: Waveland.

Tannen, D. (1998). *The argument culture: Moving from debate to dialogue*. New York: Random House.

Toulmin, S. (1958). *The uses of argument*. London: Cambridge University.

Assertiveness

✱ Alberti, R. & Emmons, M. (2001). *Your perfect right: Assertiveness and equality in your life and relationships* (8th ed.). Atascadero, CA: Impact.

Canfield, J. & Hansen, M. V. (1995). *The Aladdin Factor*. New York: Berkley.

Communication Apprehension/Speaking Anxiety

✱Dwyer, K. K. (1998). *Conquer your speechfright*. Fort Worth: Harcourt Brace.

✱ Motley, M. T. (1997). *Overcoming your fear of public speaking*. Boston: Houghton Mifflin.

✱ Richmond, V.P. & McCroskey, J. C. (1995). *Communication: Apprehension, avoidance, and effectiveness* (4th ed.) Scottsdale, AZ: Gorsuch Scarisbrick.

Conflict and Conflict Resolution

Anderson, J. W., Foster-Keuhn, M. & McKinney, B. C. (1996). *Communication skills for surviving conflicts at work*. Cresskill, NJ: Hampton.

Domenici, K. (1996). *Mediation: Empowerment in conflict management*. Prospect Heights, IL: Waveland.

✱ Folger, J. P., Poole, M. S., & Stutman, R. K. (2001). *Working through conflict: Strategies for relationships, groups and organizations* (4th ed.). New York: Longman.

✱ Janis, I. L. (1982). Groupthink: *Psychological studies of policy decisions and fiascoes* (2nd ed.). Boston: Houghton Mifflin.

✱ Littlejohn, S. W. & Domenici, K (2001). *Engaging communication in conflict: Systematic practice*. Thousand Oaks, CA: Sage.

McKinney, B. C., Kimsey, W. D., & Fuller, R. M. (1995). *Mediator communication competencies: Interpersonal communication and alternative dispute resolution* (4th ed.) Edina, MN: Burgess.

★ Wilmot, W. W. & Hocker, J. L. (2001). *Interpersonal conflict* (6th ed.). New York: McGraw-Hill.

Decision Making (See Problem Solving)

Group Communication and Team Effectiveness

Cathcart, R. S., Samovar, L. A. & Henman, L. D. (Eds), (1996). *Small group communication: Theory and practice* (7th ed.). Madison, WI: Brown & Benchmark.

★ Katzenback, J. R. & Smith, D. K. (2001). *The discipline of teams*. New York: John Wiley & Sons.

★ Katzenback, J. R. & Smith, D. K. (1993). *The wisdom of teams*. New York: John Wiley & Sons.

Kelley, R. E. (1992). *The power of followership*. New York: Doubleday.

★ LaFasto, F. & Larson, C. (2001). *When teams work best*. Thousand Oaks, CA: Sage.

★ Larson, C. & LaFasto, F. (1989). *TeamWork: What must go right/What can go wrong*. Newbury Park, CA: Sage.

Napier, R. W. & Gershenfeld, M. K. (1999). *Groups: Theory and experience* (6th ed.). Boston: Houghton Mifflin.

Robins, H & Fiunley, M. (2000). *The new why teams don't work: What goes wrong and how to make it right*. San Francisco: Berrett-Koehler.

Senge, P. M. et al. (1994). *The fifth discipline fieldbook: Strategies and tools for building a learning organization*. New York: Doubleday.

Wheelan, S. A. (1999). *Creating effective teams*. Thousand Oaks: Sage.

★ 3M Meeting Management Team with J. Drew (1994). *Mastering meetings: discovering the hidden potential of effective business meetings*. New York: McGraw-Hill.

Leadership

Barge, J. K. (1994). *Leadership: Communication skills for organizations and groups*. New York: St. Martin's.

Bennis, W. (1994). *On becoming a leader*, 2nd ed. Addison-Wesley.

★ Bennis, W. & Goldsmith, J. (1997). *Learning to lead: A workbook on becoming a leader*, 3rd ed. Cambridge, MA: Perseus.

Bennis, W. et al (2001). *The future of leadership: Today's top leadership thinkers speak to tomorrow's leaders.* San Francisco: Jossey-Bass.

★ Chemers, M. M. (1997). *An integrative theory of leaderhip*. Mahwah, NJ: Lawrence Erlbaum.

★ Hackman, M. Z. & Johnson, C. E. (2000). *Leadership: A communication perspective*, 3rd ed. Prospect Heights, IL: Waveland.

Harvard business review on leadership (1998). Harvard Business School

Kouzes, J. M. & Posner, B. Z. (1993). *Credibility: How leaders gain and lose it, why people demand it*. San Francisco: Jossey-Bass.

Northouse, P. G. (1997). *Leadership: Theory and practice*. Thousand Oaks, CA: Sage.
Resse, F. (2001). *How to lead work teams: Facilitation skills, 2nd ed.* San Francisco: Josey-Bass/Pfeiffer.
Witherspoon, P. D. (1997). *Communication leadership: An organizational perspective.* Boston: Allyn & Bacon.

Listening

★ Brownell, J. (2002). *Listening: Attitudes, principles, and skills* (2nd ed.). Boston: Allyn & Bacon.
Burley-Allen, M. (1995). *Listening: The forgotten skill* (2nd ed.). New York: John Wiley& Sons.
Nichols, M. P. (1995). *The lost art of listening*. New York: Guilford.
★ Purdy, M. & Borisoff, D. (Eds.). (1997). *Listening in everyday life* (2nd ed.). Lanham, MD: University Press of America.
Shafir, R. Z. (2000). *The zen of listening: Mindful communication in the age of distraction.* Wheaton, IL: Quest Books.
★Wolvin, A. D. & Coakley, C. G. (1996). *Listening* (5th ed.). Madison, WI: Brown & Benchmark.

Meetings

Anderson, K. (1993). *The busy manager's guide to successful meetings*. Hawthorne, NJ: Career Press.
Burleson, C. W. (1990). *Effective meetings: The complete guide*. New York: John Wiley.
Doyle, M. & Straus, D. (1976). *How to make meetings work*. New York: Jove.
Howard, V.A. & Barton, J. H. (1992). *Thinking together: Making meetings work*. New York: William Morrow.
★ Levasseur, R. E. (1994). *Breakthrough business meetings: Shared leadership in action.* Holbrook, MA: Bob Adams.
Swanson, R.A. & Knapp, B.O. (Eds.) (1991). *Innovative meeting management*. Austin, TX: 3M Meeting Management Institute.
★ 3M Meeting Management Team with J. Drew (1994). *Mastering meetings: discovering the hidden potential of effective business meetings*. New York: McGraw-Hill.

Motivation

Bowen, R. B. (2000). *Recognizing and rewarding employees*. New York: Mc-Graw-Hill.
Frazer-Robsinson, J. (1999). *Mastering motivation*. Kent, England: David Grant Publishing.
★ Hiam, A. (1999). *Motivating and rewarding employees: New and better ways to inspire your people*. Holbrook, MA: Adams Streetwise.
★ Kouzes, J. M. and Posner, B. Z. (1999). *Encouraging the heart: A leader's guide to rewarding and recognizing others*. San Francisco: Jossey-Bass.
★ Petri, H. L. (1996). *Motivation: Theory, research, and applications* (4th ed.) Pacific Grove, CA: Brooks/Cole.
★ Thomas, K. W. (2000). *Intrinsic motivation at work*. San Francisco: Barrett-Koehler.

Myers-Briggs® Type Indicator

Demarest, L. (1997). *Looking at type in the workplace*. Gainesville, FL: Center for Applications of Psychological Type.

Hirsh, S. K. (1992). *Introduction to type and teams*. Palo Alto, CA: Consulting Psychologists Press.

Isachsen, O. & Berens, L. V. (1998). *Working together*. San Juan Capistrano, CA: Institute for Management Development.

★ Kroeger, O. with Thuesen, J. M. (1992). *Type talk at work*. New York: Dell.

★ Myers, I. B. with Myers, P. B. (1990). *Gifts differing: Tenth anniversary edition*. Palo Alto, CA: Consulting Psychologists.

Nonverbal Communication

Andersen, P. A. (1999). *Nonverbal communication: Forms and functions*. Mountain View, CA: Mayfield.

Hall, E. T. (1982) *The hidden dimension*. New York: Doubleday.

Knapp, M. L. & Hall, J. A. (1997). *Nonverbal communication and interaction* (4th ed.). Fort Worth, TX: Harcourt Brace.

Remland, M. S. (2000). *Nonverbal communication in everyday life*. Boston: Houghton Mifflin.

Parliamentary Procedure

★ Jones, O. G. (1971). *Parliamentary procedure at a glance*. New York: Penguin.

Robert, H. M. with H. M. Robert, III, W. J. Evans & J. W. Cleary. (1990). *Robert's rules of order: Newly revised* (9th ed.). New York: Scott, Foresman.

Sturgis, A. (1988). *The standard code of parliamentary procedure* (3rd ed.). New York: McGraw-Hill.

Problem Solving

★ Hirokawa, R. Y. & Poole, M. S. (Eds.). (1996). *Communication and group decision making* (2nd ed.). Thousand Oaks, CA: Sage.

Howard, V. A. & Barton, J. H. (1992). *Thinking together: Making meetings work*. New York: William Morrow.

Kelly, P. K. (1994). *Team decision-making techniques: A practical guide to successful team outcomes*. Irvine, CA: Richard Chang Associates.

Also see books in the Group Communication and Team Effectiveness category.

Public/Presentation Speaking

★ Daly, J. A. & Engleberg, I. N. (2001). *Presentations in everyday life: Strategies for Effective Speaking*. Boston: Houghton Mifflin.

★ Leech, R. (1993). *How to prepare, stage, and deliver winning presentations*. New York: American Management Association.

Noonan, P. (1998). *Simply speaking: How to communicate your ideas with style, substance, and clarity*. New York: HarperCollins.

Ringle, W. J. (1998). TechEdge: *Using computers to present and persuade*. Boston: Allyn & Bacon.

Verbal Communication/Language

★ Donnellon, A. (1996). *Team talk: The power of language in team dynamics*. Boston, MA: Harvard Business School.

Ivy, D. K. & Backlund, P. (2000). *Exploring genderspeak: Personal effectiveness in gender communication* (2nd ed.). New York: McGraw-Hill.

★ Tannen, D. (1990). *You just don't understand: Women and men in conversation*. New York: William Morrow.

Virtual Groups

★ Coleman, D. (Ed.) (1997). *Groupware: Collaborative strategies for corporate LANS and Intranets*. Upper Saddle River, NJ: Prentice Hall.

Creighton, J. L. & Adams. J. W. R. (1998). *CyberMeeting: How to link people and technology in your organization*. New York: AMACOM.

★ Duarte, D. L. & Snyder, N. T. (1999). *Mastering virtual teams*. San Francisco: Jossey-Bass.

Jude-York, D. et al (2000). *Virtual teaming: Breaking the boundaries of time and place*. Menlo Park, CA: CrispLearning.

★ Lipnack, J. & Stamps, J. (2000). *Virtual teams: People working across boundaries with technology* (2nd ed.). New York: John Wiley.

★ Wood, A. F. & Smith, M. J. (2001). *Online communication: Linking technology, identity, and culture*. Mahwah, NJ: Lawrence Erlbaum.

COMMUNICATION/GROUP RESEARCH JOURNALS, NEWSLETTERS, AND HANDBOOKS

Bonito, J. A. & Hollingshead, A. B. (1997). Participation in small groups. In B. R. Burleson (Ed.), *Communication Yearbook, 20*. Thousand Oaks, CA: Sage.

Frey, L. R. (ed). (1999). *The handbook of groups communication theory and research.* Thousand Oaks, CA: Sage.

Harvard Business School. *Harvard Management Communication Letter: Tools, Techniques, and Ideas for the Articulate Executive*. A monthly publication. See Daly, J. & Engleberg, I. (1999). Coping with stagefright: How to turn terror into dynamic speaking, *Harvard Management Communication Letter*, *2* (*6*), pp. 1-4.

Hirokawa, R. Y. & Poole, M. S. (1996). *Communication and group decision making* (2nd ed.). Thousand Oaks, CA: Sage.

Small Group Research, Thousand Oaks, CA: Sage. An international journal of theory, investigation, and application.

Witte, E. & Davis, J. H. (Eds.). (1996). *Understanding group behavior: Consensual actions by small groups, Vol.1; Understanding group behavior: Small group processes and interpersonal relations, Vol. 2*. Mahway, NJ: Lawrence Erlbaum.

Assessment Options for Graded Assignments

PROBLEM SOLVING DISCUSSION

GOAL

- To make a group decision using The Standard Agenda approach to problem solving.

PARTICIPANTS

Your group will consist of 5 to 7 members. Exchange phone numbers and/or email addresses.

DISCUSSION QUESTION REQUIREMENTS

The group should select a problem that needs to be solved as the discussion topic. The topic should be worded as a question of policy.

AGENDA REQUIREMENTS

The group should develop a discussion agenda. It should conform to The Standard Agenda approach to problem solving presented in the textbook. The agenda should be typed and copies distributed to the instructor and all group members.

BIBLIOGRAPHY REQUIREMENTS

Each member should research and collect information on the topic. These materials should be brought to class for use during the discussion. On the day of the discussion, each group member should turn in a bibliography with a minimum of five sources.

DISCUSSION REQUIREMENTS

A group discussion is not a series of individual speeches. Discussion requires interaction among group members. As the group prepares for this assignment, members should not discuss the content of the discussion. During the discussion members should direct their comments to fellow group members. The discussion will last approximately 40 minutes.

EVALUATION REQUIREMENTS

After the group discussion, group members should complete and turn in a post-meeting reaction (PMR) form. On days that groups are not scheduled to participate in a discussion, they will observe other group discussions and complete assessment forms.

GRADING CRITERIA

A portion of your grade will be a shared group grade based on the following items:

- agenda preparation
- ability to follow the agenda
- management of discussion time
- ability to use The Standard Agenda approach
- communication climate
- overall quality of discussion

The remaining portion of your grade will be based on your individual performance of the following items:

- leadership skills
- participation skills
- listening behavior
- preparation and use of information
- contribution of ideas and information
- individual bibliography
- completion of evaluation forms

GROUP PRESENTATION PROJECT

GOALS

- To prepare and present a public group presentation.
- To demonstrate the ability to follow the oral presentation guidelines discussed in the textbook.

PARTICIPANTS

Your group will consist of 4 to 6 members. Exchange phone numbers and/or email addresses.

TOPIC REQUIREMENTS

The group should select a topic that it believes would be interesting to the class. It is also important that all group members find the topic worthwhile. After choosing a broad topic, the group should divide the topic into subtopics that can be divided among group members for individual oral presentations.

PURPOSE

Develop a purpose statement for your presentation. What do you want the class to know, believe, or do as a result of the presentation?

BIBLIOGRAPHIC REQUIREMENTS

The group should agree upon a plan for collecting information. Each group member will be responsible for researching a different aspect of the topic. In addition, all group members should be informed about the broad topic. On the day of the discussion, each group member will turn in a bibliography with a minimum of five sources.

OUTLINE REQUIREMENTS

The group must develop an outline for its oral presentation that should conform to the format presented in the textbook. The outline should be typed and copies distributed to the instructor and all group members.

PRESENTATION REQUIREMENTS

Group members should deliver a coordinated oral presentation to the class on the assigned day. All members should use an extemporaneous form of delivery. Group members should not read from a manuscript. The group presentation should include the use of at least three visual aids. The group will have 30 minutes to complete the presentation.

EVALUATION REQUIREMENTS

Each group is responsible for developing its own post-meeting reaction (PMR) form for the day of the presentation. Each member should complete a copy of the form immediately after the group has delivered its oral presentations to the class. On days that your group is not scheduled to present, you will observe other groups' presentations and complete assessment forms.

GRADING CRITERIA

A portion of your grade will be a shared group grade based on the following items:

- clear presentation of purpose
- adaptation to listeners
- adaptation to setting
- organization of the overall group presentation
- group presentation outline
- ability to work as a coordinated team
- overall quality of the group presentation
- development of the PMR form

The remaining portion of your grade will be based on your individual performance on the following items:

- adaptation to listeners
- adaptation to setting
- use of information and ideas
- organization of your portion(s) of the presentation
- personal credibility
- individual delivery of your portion(s) of the presentation
- individual bibliography
- completion of evaluation forms

REAL WORLD GROUP PRESENTATION

GOALS

- To prepare and present a team presentation to one or more real-world critical decision makers.
- To accept the roles and responsibilities of working with others on a real team.

PARTICPANTS

Your group will consist of 5 to 7 members. This is a major assignment. Thus, your group should begin planning its presentation as soon as possible. Your instructor may provide some in-class time for your group to prepare. However, your group should make arrangements to meet with each other outside of class to prepare and practice your presentation. Every group member must participate in the final presentation.

TOPIC REQUIREMENTS

Each group should prepare a presentation related to a campus or community concern. Groups should plan to explain the problem to critical decision makers and present recommendations for solutions. The topic must be approved by the instructor.

Examples: What should be done to improve class registration?
How can local citizens help take a "bite out of crime"?

RESEARCH

The group must base its presentation and recommendations on relevant research. Research must include interviews with relevant college and community officials as well as surveys and/or interviews with students or community members.

AGENDA

The group must develop an agenda for the presentation. The agenda must be typed and copies distributed to the instructor, the entire class, and the audience of decision makers. Each group member must develop an outline for their individual presentations.

PRESENTATION REQUIREMENTS

The group should deliver a well-prepared and thoroughly rehearsed presentation. Presentations may take place in the classroom or in the decision makers' offices. All presenters should use an extemporaneous delivery. The group's presentation should include at least three presentation aids. Each group will have 30 minutes for the presentation to be followed by a 15-minute question-and-answer session.

GRADING CRITERIA

A portion of your grade will be a shared group grade based on the following:

- sufficient and appropriate research
- effective integration of the research into the presentation
- clear explanations and documentation of research
- clear presentation of purpose
- adaptation to the audience
- adaptation to the setting
- organization of the overall group presentation
- seamlessness of group presentation
- quality of presentation aids
- submission of written materials

A portion of your grade will be based on your individual performance on the following:

- cooperation with other members during the planning process
- sufficient and appropriate research
- effective use of research in the individual presentation
- clear explanation and documentation of research
- submission of written materials
- clear presentation of purpose
- adaptation to the audience
- adaptation to the setting
- organization of the individual presentation
- effectiveness of delivery

GROUP ANALYSIS PAPER

ASSIGNMENT

You will be assigned to work with a group on an ongoing basis to prepare a group presentation and/or conduct a problem-solving discussion. In addition to participating in the group assignment, you will write a paper analyzing your group's effectiveness. You may want to take notes about members' behaviors after each group meeting in order to recall specific examples for inclusion in your paper. Your paper will be due after the group assignment has been completed.

ISSUES FOR ANALYSIS

Your analysis of the group should address five issues. Provide specific examples of group behavior to support your conclusions.

Group Development

Using either Tuckman's stages or Fisher's phases, discuss the development of your group. How useful were Tuckman's stages or Fisher's phases in accurately describing group development?

Norms And Roles

Identify your group's norms. Discuss any deviation from those norms. Identify member roles. Discuss the distribution of task, maintenance, and self-centered roles.

Leadership

Did your group appoint a leader or did a leader emerge? Using one of the theories discussed in the textbook, describe and analyze the leadership in your group.

Participation

Using the Myers-Briggs® personality type theory or Schultz's FIRO theory, try to identify each group member's personality type or interpersonal needs. Did conflicting personalities create any problems for the group?

Group Outcomes

Discuss how effectively or ineffectively the group performed. If you were to work with this group again, what strategies could you use to improve group performance?

TWELVE ANGRY MEN ANALYSIS PAPER

ASSIGNMENT OVERVIEW

View the film *Twelve Angry Men* and write a paper analyzing the group discussion dramatized in the film. While watching the film, take notes that will provide you with specific examples to illustrate concepts related to small group communication. You may want to rent the film from a local video store and view it again as you develop ideas for your paper.

ISSUES FOR ANALYSIS

Your analysis of the group should address five issues. Provide specific examples from the film to support your conclusions.

Leadership

Describe the different approaches to leadership represented on the jury. What theory or theories best explain(s) the leadership of this group?

Participation

Describe the task, maintenance, and self-centered roles represented in the film. What were some of the participation problems confronted by the group? How did the group deal with these problems?

Climate

Describe the communication climate throughout most of the jury's deliberations. What specific verbal and nonverbal behaviors contributed to this climate?

Conflict

Provide examples of substantive, procedural, and affective conflict. What were some of the conflict styles of group members? How successfully were conflicts resolved in the group?

Argumentation

Evaluate the jury members' arguments. How well did the characters evaluate information?

GROUPWORK LOG

ASSIGNMENT OVERVIEW

Throughout this course, you will work in many groups. Some groups may meet on an ongoing basis to prepare for a graded assignment. Other group experiences will occur during in-class activities. Keep a log of your experiences throughout the course. You will need a journal or notebook to record your thoughts.

LOG ENTRY GUIDELINES

The following elements should be included in most of your log entries. In addition, you may choose to record any other thoughts or observations regarding a particular group experience.

- After each group meeting, discussion, or activity, record an entry into your log.
- Identify the purpose, or goal, of the group experience.
- Identify the group outcome. What decisions were made or goals accomplished?
- Describe your level of satisfaction with the group. Was the communication climate supportive? What problems existed? Were problems dealt with appropriately? What was your contribution to the group?
- Explain what you learned as a result of working with the group. How can you use the experience to improve your next group encounter? What, if anything, could this group have done better to improve the experience?

DECISION MAKING COMPETENCIES

Directions: Rate the group as a whole in terms of how well it solved problems and made decisions.

Name of group: ________________________

Comments:

	Superior	Satisfactory	Unsatisfactory
1. DEFINES/ANALYZES PROBLEMS. Appropriately defines and analyzes the problem that confronts the group.			
2. IDENTIFIES CRITERIA. Appropriately participates in the establishment of the group goal and identifies criteria for assessing the quality of the group outcome.			
3. GENERATES SOLUTIONS. Appropriately identifies the solutions or alternatives identified by group members.			
4. EVALUATES SOLUTIONS. Appropriately evaluates the solutions or alternatives identified by the group members.			
5. MAINTAINS TASK FOCUS. Appropriately helps the group stay on the task, issue, or agenda item the group is discussing.			
6. MANAGES CONFLICT. Appropriately manages disagreements and conflicts.			
7. MAINTAINS CLIMATE. Appropriately provides supportive comments to other group members.			
8. MANAGES INTERACTION. Helps manage interaction and appropriately invites others to participate.			

PARTICIPATION ASSESSMENT INSTRUMENT

Name of Group Member ______________________________

Directions: Use the following items to evaluate the quantity and quality of the participation by the individual members of your group. Write a summary assessment on the back of this form.

1. Contribution to the group's task function. (Provides or asks for information and opinions, initiates discussion, clarifies, summarizes, evaluates, energizes, etc.

5	4	3	2	1
Excellent		Average		Poor

2. Contribution to the group's maintenance functions. (Serves as encourager, harmonizer, compromiser, tension releaser, gatekeeper, standards monitor, observer, follower, etc.)

5	4	3	2	1
Excellent		Average		Poor

3. Contribution to effective and efficient group process. (Avoids self-centered roles, follows the agenda, respects and adapts to member traits and differences, etc.)

5	4	3	2	1
Excellent		Average		Poor

4. Readiness to contribute. (Well- prepared)

5	4	3	2	1
Excellent		Average		Poor

5. Willingness to contribute. (Level of commitment to group's goal; willingness to share, listen, adapt, exercise responsibility, etc.)

5	4	3	2	1
Excellent		Average		Poor

6. Ability to contribute. (Communication skills and technical skills)

5	4	3	2	1
Excellent		Average		Poor

7. Ability to deal with difficulties. (Apathy, deviant members, hidden agendas, etc.)

5	4	3	2	1
Excellent		Average		Poor

8. Overall Effectiveness.

5	4	3	2	1
Excellent		Average		Poor

POST-MEETING REACTION (PMR) FORM

NAME OF EVALUATOR:____

Directions: After a selected meeting, complete the following PMR form by circling the number that best represents the answer to each question. After compiling the answers from all participants, including the chairperson, use the results as a base for improving future meetings.

1. How clear was the purpose of the meeting?

   Unclear 1 2 3 4 5 Clear

2. How clear was the agenda?

   Unclear 1 2 3 4 5 Clear

3. How well was the agenda followed?

   Not followed 1 2 3 4 5 Followed

4. How conducive was the meeting room for the purpose?

   Not conducive 1 2 3 4 5 Conducive

5. How prepared were group members for the meeting?

   Unprepared 1 2 3 4 5 Prepared

6. Did everyone have an equal opportunity to participate in the discussion?

   Limited Opportunity 1 2 3 4 5 Ample Opportunity

7. Were different viewpoints listened to?

   Not listened to 1 2 3 4 5 Listened to

8. How would you describe the overall climate of the meeting?

   Hostile 1 2 3 4 5 Friendly

9. Were assignments and deadlines made clear by the end of the meeting?

   Unclear 1 2 3 4 5 Clear

10. How would you rate this meeting overall?

   Unproductive 1 2 3 4 5 Productive

Additional Comments:

ORAL PRESENTATION SCALE

Member: ______________________________

Topic or Purpose of Oral Presentation: ______________________________

PRESENTATION GUIDELINES	Superior	Satisfactory	Unsatisfactory
PURPOSE: Clear and reasonable goal.			
AUDIENCE: Adapts to listeners.			
LOGISTICS: Adapts to occasion and setting.			
CONTENT: Uses a variety of effective supporting materials.			
ORGANIZATION: Clear organization; effective introduction and conclusion; clear language.			
CREDIBILITY: Competence and character.			
PERFORMANCE: Uses voice, body, and visual aids effectively.			

COMMENTS:

Strengths of Oral Presentation:

Suggestions for Improvement:

Groupwork: Activities for Working in Groups

INITIAL CLASS MEETINGS

AUTOGRAPH HUNT

GOALS

- To provide students with a fun and efficient way to meet their classmates.
- To discover the various types of groups in which students have worked.

PARTICIPANTS

Entire class

PROCEDURE

1. Distribute copies of the *Autograph Hunt* handout to all students.
2. Explain that the goal is to get acquainted with other students as they collect autographs of classmates who have been members of the groups listed on the handout. Explain the following guidelines:
   - You may not autograph your own handout.
   - Individuals who have been a member of more than one of the groups listed on the handout should choose only one item to autograph.
   - Ask questions about an individual's experiences with a particular group. Find out when he or she was a member and for how long, the types of activities the group did, and whether the group was effective. Do not simply collect an autograph and move to the next person.
   - After each conversation, move on to the next person. Try to collect as many autographs as you can.
3. Instruct everyone to stand and begin moving around the room to collect autographs.

TEACHING TIPS

If there is not enough time for everyone to complete all the categories, suggest that they continue collecting autographs right before the next class meeting. Follow this activity with a discussion of the many different types of groups represented in class. Discussion questions:

- ❖ To which groups did almost everyone belong?
- ❖ Which groups were more difficult to get autographed?
- ❖ What were some of the unique groups represented in the class?
- ❖ How important do you think working in groups is in our personal, community, and work lives?
- ❖ What can you conclude about the extent and nature of group communication?

AUTOGRAPH HUNT

Instructions: Collect autographs from classmates who have been members of the groups on this list. An individual may sign your sheet in only one category.

	I am/was a member of . . .	Autograph	Comments
1.	a large family.		
2.	a fraternity or sorority.		
3.	an athletic team.		
4.	Boy or Girl Scouts.		
5.	the military.		
6.	a campus club.		
7.	student government.		
8.	a self-help group.		
9.	a book discussion group.		
10.	a class study group.		
11.	a religious study group.		
12.	a jury.		
13.	a community service organization.		
14.	a labor union.		
15.	an on-line chat group.		
16.	a band.		
17.	a theatrical production.		
18.	a committee at work.		
19.	a choir.		
20.	Other (Find a member of a unique group.)		

INITIAL CLASS MEETINGS

WHY ARE YOU TAKING THIS COURSE?

GOALS

- To identify the group skills students seek to develop.
- To develop student goal statements for the course.

PARTICIPANTS

Groups of 5 to 7 members

PROCEDURE

1. Distribute the *Why Are You Taking This Course?* handout in class.
2. Ask students to complete parts one and two of the form. Give students sufficient time to think about the questions and write their responses.
3. Divide the class into groups to discuss their answers to parts one and two. Suggest that they discuss the following questions:
   - What reasons do we share for taking this course?
   - What unique reasons did some members identify for taking this course?
   - What do we hope to learn from this course?
4. Following discussion of their individual answers, ask the groups to identify at least three common goals that they want to accomplish by taking this course. The groups should write their goal statements on part three of this handout.
5. Ask each group to appoint a spokesperson to present the group's goals to the entire class.

TEACHING TIPS

This activity gives students an opportunity to express their goals and attitudes about a small group communication course. Compiling, distributing, and using such interest as the basis for class discussion can reassure students that the course will meet their needs and address their concerns. In addition, the list of student answers can be used to preview and highlight topics that will be covered in the course. Sometimes an unusual answer can trigger an interesting in-class discussion. Discussion questions:

❖ To what extent are their goals similar to or different from others in the class?
❖ What can they do to maximize their chances of meeting their goals?

WHY ARE YOU TAKING THIS COURSE?

Name:____

PART I: I AM TAKING THIS COURSE BECAUSE . . .

Check the item(s) that accurately completes the statement.

Are you taking this course ...

- ❒ . . . because you *want* to?
- ❒ . . . because you *need* to?
- ❒ . . . because you *have* to?

PART II: MY REASONS FOR TAKING THIS COURSE

Explain or list the reasons you are taking this course.

PART III: GROUP GOAL STATEMENTS

After discussing the individual answers to the above items, the group should identify at least three common goals that students hope to accomplish as a result of taking this course. (This part is to be completed as a group.)

1. We hope to . . .

2. We hope to . . .

3. We hope to . . .

INITIAL CLASS MEETINGS

GETTING ACQUAINTED

GOAL

- To get to know group members in an efficient and meaningful way.

PARTICIPANTS

Groups of 5 to 7 members

PROCEDURE

1. Distribute the *Get Acquainted Statements* handout in class.
2. Beginning with statement 1, each group member completes the statement in turn before going on to statement 2. Let a different person begin each round of statement completions. The group will have 30 minutes to complete the statements.
3. Try to be as open and honest as possible. If you feel uncomfortable or unable to complete a statement, say "I pass" and go on to the next person.
4. It is not necessary to complete all of the statements during the allotted time.

TEACHING TIPS

You may add or subtract statements to create a list more appropriate for your students and your instructional needs. It is important to create a friendly, nonevaluative climate for this activity in order to enhance trust and acceptance among group members.
Discussion questions:

❖ Did the exercise help you get to know other group members?
❖ Why is it difficult to get to know other people without such an exercise?
❖ Which statements were the most difficult to complete?
❖ How do you feel about your group and its members?

GET ACQUAINTED STATEMENTS

1. My name is . . .

2. I am taking this course because . . .

3. When I am in a new group, I . . .

4. Two words that describe me are . . .

5. It is frustrating to work in groups when . . .

6. When I have free time, I like to . . .

7. A good group member should . . .

8. When someone disagrees with me, I . . .

9. An effective group leader should . . .

10. This experience has made me feel . . .

INITIAL CLASS MEETINGS

THE DINNER PARTY

GOAL

- To create an atmosphere in which sharing is accepted and encouraged.
- To allow students to get to know one another.

PARTICIPANTS

Groups of 5 to 6 members

PROCEDURE

1. Tell students that they are each to host a dinner party. They may select any 5 people, living or dead, to attend that party. They may not invite friends or family members. Give them a few minutes to make their selections.
2. Divide the students into groups of 5 to 6 people and have them share their lists with the others. Ask them to explain the reasoning behind their choices.
3. You may choose to have a spokesperson report the guest list generated by members of each group to the class.

TEACHING TIPS

This exercise allows students to find out something more about each other without any need for direct personal disclosures. You may choose to substitute other scenarios such as "You have been given an all-expense paid trip anywhere in the world for 2 weeks. Where would you go?" "If you could travel on a time machine to any period in history, what would it be and why?" Discussion questions:

- ❖ Did you select any of the same guests as anyone else? How did that affect your perceptions of that person?
- ❖ Were there any choices that surprised you? Why?
- ❖ Were there any guests selected whom you would not have in your home?
- ❖ Would you change your mind about your choices after hearing what others had to say?
- ❖ What did you learn about others in your group?

CHAPTER I

INTRODUCTION TO SMALL GROUP COMMUNICATION

IT WAS THE BEST OF GROUPS; IT WAS THE WORST OF GROUPS

GOALS

- To identify advantages and disadvantages of working in groups.
- To demonstrate the number and different types of groups to which students belong.
- To provide students with the opportunity to share their past group experiences with other students.

PARTICIPANTS

Groups of 5 to 7 members.

PROCEDURE

This exercise is provided in the Groupwork section of the chapter.

1. Ask students to think about some of the groups in which they have worked. Students should consider groups in which they liked working as well as the groups they disliked. Ask them to identify the characteristics that were unique to the best groups and which were unique to the worst groups. Have them write down at least two characteristics for each type of group.
2. Divide the class into groups. Distribute *It was the Best of Groups; It was the Worst of Groups* worksheet.
3. Have students take turns in the group, explaining one unique characteristic for each type of group. Encourage them to tell stories about their experiences.
4. Groups should then record on the worksheet as many unique characteristics of the best and worst groups and be prepared to discuss them in class.

TEACHING TIPS

This activity can be conducted prior to the discussion of the advantages and disadvantages of working in groups that is presented in the textbook. Discussion questions:

❖ What are the major factors contributing to positive experiences?
❖ What are the major factors contributing to negative experiences?
❖ Do the positive experiences of working in groups outweigh the advantages, or vice versa?
❖ How can groups avoid engaging in the behaviors that were perceived as the worst characteristics?

IT WAS THE BEST OF GROUPS; IT WAS THE WORST OF GROUPS

	THE BEST OF GROUPS	THE WORST OF GROUPS
1.		
2.		
3.		
4.		
5.		
6.		
7.		
8.		
9.		
10.		

CHAPTER 1

INTRODUCTION TO SMALL GROUP COMMUNICATION

SPEAK YOUR MIND ABOUT COLLEGE

GOALS

- To help students understand the variables that enhance student success.
- To provide an initial group exercise that relies on student expertise and experience.

PARTICIPANTS

The entire class and groups of 5 to 7 members

PROCEDURE

1. Introduce Richard Light's *Making the Most of College: Students Speak Their Minds*—its purpose, methodology, and importance to student success.
2. Distribute the *Students Speak Their Minds* handout. Give students time to read and think about these suggestions.
3. Ask students to rank each of the suggestions in terms of their importance to achieving success in college.
4. Divide the class into groups of 5 to 7 members. Each group should answer the following questions based on member beliefs and experiences:
   - Which suggestions are most important to achieving student success?
   - Which suggestions are least important to achieving student success?
   - To what extent do the suggestions of Harvard University students apply to you?
5. Each group should report to the class about the suggestions they thought were most important, least important, or not applicable.
6. At the end of the discussion, take a few minutes to discuss how class members will use the suggestions.

TEACHING TIPS

The suggestions in Richard Light's book are based on ten years of systematic interviews with more than 1,000 Harvard University students. As an educational statistician, he drew conclusions from the interviews bolstered by educational research and personal experience. In addition to suggestions from students, Light's book also provides suggestions for faculty, advisors, and college administrations. See Light, R. J. (2001). *Making the Most of College: Students Speak their Minds*. Cambridge, MA: Harvard University Press. Discussion questions:

- ❖ Were any of these suggestions ones you had not thought much about?
- ❖ Have you already made special efforts in any of these areas? If so, what impact did it have on your learning?
- ❖ Are there any specific changes you intend to make in the future?

STUDENTS SPEAK THEIR MINDS*

The following advice for *making the most of college* is based on interviews with more than 1,000 students who attended Harvard University during a ten-year period. As you read these suggestions, rank (1st, 2nd, 3rd) and rate how you value this advice.

Rank	Student Success Suggestions	Absolutely important	Important	Somewhat important	Moderately important	Not at all important
	Time Management					
	Outside Involvement					
	Seek and Get Help					
	Study Groups					
	Interact with "Others"					
	Small Classes					
	Speak and Write					
	Active Student					

1. **Learn time management skills**. Organize your work for class. Allot regular and sufficient time for classes, study, and homework.

2. **Get involved** in at least one activity other than taking courses. Work, volunteer in the community, or participate in college activities and programs.

3. **Seek and get help** when you need it. Seek advice from a professor, a counselor, an advisor, or a staff member. Find out about study skills classes, free tutoring, college regulations, scholarships, loans, and college activities.

4. **Study in groups**. Study outside of class in small study groups. By studying with others, you will learn from others and become a more motivated student.

5. **Interact with "other" students.** Get to know students, faculty, and staff who represent different races, nationalities, ages, life styles, and religions.

6. **Enroll in small classes** even if means taking a course at a non-prime class hour or specialized classes such as Honors curses or an upper-level elective.

7. **Improve your speaking and writing skills**. Students who speak and write well are more likely to succeed. If you have difficultly speaking or writing, seek help from an instructor or sign up for tutoring sessions in the college's writing center.

8. **Be an active student in class**. Listen carefully and take useful notes. Ask questions in class. Meet with your professor. Use the writing center, tutoring center, and counseling center for help. Ask others to read and comment on your assignments.

*Light, R. J. (2001) *Making the Most of College: Students Speak their Minds*. Cambridge, MA: Harvard University Press.

CHAPTER 1

INTRODUCTION TO SMALL GROUP COMMUNICATION

HOW BIG IS SMALL?

GOAL

- To discover how the size of a group influences interaction.

PARTICIPANTS

Initially, groups of 3 members.

PROCEDURE

1. Divide the class into groups of three. Distribute a copy of the case study entitled *Benched.* Instruct the groups to discuss the case and answer the final questions.
2. After five minutes, combine each group with another group. Instruct the groups of six members to continue discussing the case.
3. After five minutes, combine the groups of six with other groups of six to continue discussing the case. Continue combining groups every five minutes until the entire class is seated in a circle in one large group.
4. As one large group, the class should continue discussing the case for five minutes.

TEACHING TIPS

This activity allows students to experience the differences in interaction between small and large groups. Their answers to the case study questions are not important in this activity. In fact, any case or problem can be substituted for the one provided. Follow the activity with a class discussion about group size. Discussion questions:

❖ In which size group were you most comfortable?
❖ Which size group contributed the most diverse viewpoints during the discussion?
❖ Which size group allowed you to feel you had a sufficient opportunity to participate?
❖ Which size group would you choose if you were assigned an important project that required a group to meet frequently and complete many important tasks? Why?
❖ Why is 5 to 7 members considered the ideal size for a problem-solving discussion?

CASE STUDY: BENCHED

For eight years the managers of a computer technology firm have been getting together once a month to play basketball. The games have been an opportunity for everyone to socialize and further develop working relationships. The managers have also found that some business matters are worked out when they meet in this informal atmosphere. As a result, all of the managers believe that the games are important, not only as a recreational activity but as a way to enhance business teamwork.

Until recently, all of the managers were male. Last month Wanda was promoted to a management position. Wanda does not play basketball. She worries that she may be left "out of the loop" on some business matters by not associating with her colleagues in this informal setting.

What is the problem in this situation? What are the implications for Wanda and her colleagues if she doesn't participate in the basketball games? What should Wanda do? What should the other managers do?

CHAPTER I

INTRODUCTION TO SMALL GROUP COMMUNICATION

PIECES OF A PUZZLE

GOAL

- To demonstrate that groups can often accomplish more than individuals working alone.
- To demonstrate the advantage of pooling group resources.

PARTICIPANTS

Groups of 5 to 7 members.

PROCEDURE

1. Before class, the instructor should create several puzzles by using pictures from magazines or greeting cards. Cut several pictures into seven pieces each. Small children's puzzles will also work for this activity. You will need enough puzzles to supply every member of the class with at least one piece of the puzzle.
2. Give each class member a piece of a puzzle. Make sure that all of the puzzle pieces are distributed. You may need to give some students two pieces. Make sure that both pieces are parts of the same puzzle.
3. Instruct students to stand and begin looking for group members with other parts of the same puzzle.

TEACHING TIPS

This is a quick and simple activity that demonstrates the value of each member's contribution to a group. Try to distribute pieces of the same puzzle to students who are not sitting near each other. This activity is easily paired with another activity as a creative way to assign members to groups. Discussion questions:

- ❖ What would happen if one member could not find his or her group? Would the group have been able to complete the task?
- ❖ What is the value of an individual's piece of the puzzle when it is not combined with contributions from the rest of the group?
- ❖ Why do groups tend to outperform individuals working alone?

CHAPTER 2

GROUP FORMATION AND DEVELOPMENT

CLASSROOM NORMS

GOAL

- To understand the purpose and impact of implicit and explicit norms.

PARTICIPANTS

Groups of 5 to 7 members.

PROCEDURE

This exercise is provided in the Groupwork section of the chapter.

1. Each group should generate a list of the implicit and explicit norms that operate in the classroom.
   - Example of implicit norm: When students come in late, they tip-toe to the first available seat near the door.
   - Example of explicit norm: The syllabus states that no make-up work will be allowed if students do not have legitimate, written excuses.
2. Each group should rank the norms on each list in terms of their usefulness in ensuring quality instruction and effective learning.
3. Groups should post their lists and compare them to the norms generated by other groups.

TEACHING TIPS

This activity works well after students are familiar with group norms. Discussion questions:

- ❖ Do any norms appear on all or most lists?
- ❖ Which norms are most important?
- ❖ What impact would failure to follow these norms have on the educational process?
- ❖ Are there more implicit than explicit norms?
- ❖ How are classroom norms different than private group norms?
- ❖ Should any of the norms be changed, strengthened, or abolished in this class?

CHAPTER 2

GROUP FORMATION AND DEVELOPMENT

MEETING NEEDS

GOALS

- To review Maslow's Hierarchy of Needs.
- To discover different ways in which groups fulfill basic needs.

PARTICIPANTS

Groups of 5 to 7 members.

PROCEDURE

1. Review the five human needs identified by Abraham Maslow.
2. Divide the class into small groups.
3. Instruct students to discuss the ways in which membership in groups can fulfill each need.
4. Ask each group to identify at least three examples of how groups can satisfy each of Maslow's needs.
5. Each group should appoint a spokesperson to present its examples to the entire class for discussion.

TEACHING TIPS

This activity should help students develop a better understanding of the distinctions between each of the needs as well as how groups can fulfill them. The examples that students present can be a springboard for an interesting class discussion. Discussion questions:

❖ Why are some needs more important than others?
❖ How do groups fulfill some of those needs?
❖ Do some groups fulfill more than one need?
❖ What might happen if a group fails to fulfill a member's needs?

CHAPTER 2

GROUP FORMATION AND DEVELOPMENT

UNFULFILLED FIRO NEEDS

GOALS

- To review William Schutz's Fundamental Interpersonal Relationship Orientation (FIRO) theory.
- To demonstrate the potential behavior of individuals whose needs are unmet.

PARTICIPANTS

Groups of 5 to 7 members.

PROCEDURE

1. Before class prepare copies of the *FIRO Behaviors* handout. One copy per group is sufficient. Cut the member descriptions into individual strips.
2. Divide the class into groups. Provide each member with a strip of paper describing the behavior he or she is to perform during the group discussion.
3. Inform students that they will participate in a group discussion in which they should behave in a way that is consistent with the description they have been assigned. Group members should not reveal their assigned behavior to others. Students should be given a few minutes to think about the descriptions and the behavioral role they will play.
4. Instruct groups to discuss the following question for about ten minutes: "Should the insanity defense be permitted in criminal trials?"
5. After the group discussions, ask the members to guess what other members' needs are and whether those needs were unfulfilled.

TEACHING TIPS

You may choose to modify the activity by assigning only the behaviors of members whose interpersonal needs are unfulfilled. The groups could then engage in the discussion a second time using the behaviors of social members, democratic members, and personal members. This variation allows students to recognize the difference between fulfilled and unfulfilled needs. Follow the activity with a discussion of Schutz's FIRO theory. Discussion questions:

- ❖ Were you able to guess the unfulfilled needs of other members?
- ❖ What experiences have you had in the past with unfulfilled needs?
- ❖ What could the group do to encourage other members to change their behavior?

FIRO BEHAVIORS

IDEAL SOCIAL MEMBER

Your inclusion needs have been met. You enjoy working with people. You have a strong commitment to the group and its goals. You feel valued and appreciated.

UNDERSOCIAL MEMBER

Your inclusion needs have not been met. You feel unworthy and undervalued by the group. You tend to withdraw from the discussion. You do not volunteer or cooperate. You avoid attracting attention by remaining quiet.

OVERSOCIAL MEMBER

Your inclusion needs have not been met. You seek attention from the group to compensate for your feelings of inadequacy. You try to impress others with what and who you know.

DEMOCRATIC MEMBER

Your control needs have been met. You have no problems with power and control. You are comfortable giving and receiving orders. You are often a group leader. You feel that other members see you as competent and trustworthy.

ABDICRAT

Your control needs have not been met. You have no hope of controlling the group. You tend to be submissive. You avoid responsibilities but will do what you are told.

AUTOCRAT

Your control needs have not been met. You try to dominate the group. You may criticize other members and force them to accept your ideas. You don't trust the other members.

IDEAL PERSONAL MEMBER

Your affection needs have been met. You have no emotional problems when dealing with other members. You have a personal commitment to improving the group's social and emotional climate.

UNDERPERSONAL MEMBER

Your affection needs have not been met. You don't believe that the other members like you. You only form superficial relationships within the group. You rarely reveal your honest feelings or opinions. You appear aloof and uninvolved.

OVERPERSONAL MEMBER

Your affection needs have not been met. You try to get close to everyone. You seek relationships with others even though they aren't interested. You are too talkative, too personal, and too confiding.

CHAPTER 2

GROUP FORMATION AND DEVELOPMENT

GROUP EXPECTATIONS

GOAL

- To explore different types of group norms.
- To begin establishing norms for the group.

PARTICIPANTS

Groups of 5 to 7 members.

PROCEDURE

1. Review with the class the four categories of group norms discussed in Chapter 2 of the textbook.
2. Ask groups to develop a list of communication behaviors that will be acceptable in the group and a list that will be unacceptable. "We will respectfully listen to all members ideas" is an example of an interaction norm.
3. Next, students should discuss how they will conduct their group meetings throughout the semester. "Our meetings will last no longer than one hour" is an example of a procedural norm.
4. Groups should then discuss how members will gain influence and earn the respect of their fellow group members. "Group members earn influence in the group by being committed and reliable" is an example of a status norm.
5. Finally, the group should discuss the quantity and quality of work expected from each member. "Members should expect to devote three hours of work a week to the group" is an example of an achievement norm.
6. After groups have developed a list of norms for each category have them narrow the list to only the norms the group chooses to actually adopt.
7. A spokesperson from each group should present the norms to the class.

TEACHING TIPS

This activity is best conducted within groups that have already been formed to work on a graded assignment for the course. This activity requires groups to develop explicit norms. However, some of these norms usually develop as implicit norms. Allow groups to struggle with those issues and plan to address them during the discussion. Discussion questions:

- ❖ What were some of the norms adopted by most of the groups? Did any group establish a unique norm?
- ❖ What norms were the most difficult to establish?
- ❖ Would it be more appropriate for some of these norms to instead develop as implicit norms? If so, which ones?
- ❖ Did the groups establish realistic norms? Which ones will be difficult to follow? What impact would failure to follow those norms have on the group?

CHAPTER 3

PARTICIPATION IN GROUPS

TYPE TALK IN GROUPS

GOAL

- To understand how Myers-Briggs® type preferences can impact group perceptions and interaction.

PARTICIPANTS

Groups of 4 or 5 members.

PROCEDURE

This exercise is provided in the Groupwork section of the chapter.

1. Based on the chapter and the descriptive words listed in the following table, group members should select the four types that they believe best describe their own preferences and personalities.
2. Group members should also determine which types, in their opinions, best describe the personalities of other group members.
3. Upon completing this step, everyone should share their perceptions with the rest of the group including their own four preferences.
4. Discuss the extent to which member perceptions match one another.

TEACHING TIPS

Your campus testing or counseling center may have staff members qualified to conduct a more accurate Myers-Briggs® assessment. If so, it may be worthwhile for your students to receive a more complete assessment prior to completing this activity.

Discussion questions:

❖ To what extent and why is there agreement or disagreement among members on type preference?

❖ Is the group missing any of the types?

❖ How could the absence of one or more types affect group interaction and productivity?

❖ Did the group accurately perceive your preferences as you see them? Which of your group behaviors may have contributed to the accurate or inaccurate perceptions?

❖ If you are interested in obtaining more information about Myers-Briggs® type preferences and assessment instruments, contact CAPT at:

Center for the Applications of Psychological Type
2815 NW 13th Street, Suite 401
Gainesville, Florida 32609
1-800-777-2278

MYERS-BRIGGS® TYPE PREFERENCES

Extrovert. Outgoing; speaks then thinks, sociable; likes groups.	**Introvert.** Private; thinks then speaks, reflective; prefers to work alone.
Sensor. Focuses on details; factual, practical, realistic; likes facts	**Intuitive**. Focuses on the big picture; theoretical, gets bored with facts/details.
Thinker. Task-oriented, objective, firm, analytical, detached	**Feeler.** People-oriented, subjective, humane, appreciative, involved.
Judger. Well-organized, structured, in control, definite; likes deadlines	**Perceiver.** Flexible, goes-with-the-flow; dislikes deadlines; spontaneous.

CHAPTER 3

PARTICIPATION IN GROUPS

FUNCTIONAL ROLE PLAYING

GOALS

- To experience and observe task, maintenance, and self-centered roles in a group.
- To become aware of the negative influence of self-centered roles.

PARTICIPANTS

Groups of 5 to 7 members.

PROCEDURE

1. Before class, prepare copies of the *Functional Roles* handout. One copy should be sufficient for a class of 25 students or less. Cut the role descriptions into individual pieces.
2. Divide the class into groups. Provide each member with a piece of paper describing the role he or she is to perform during a group discussion.
3. Inform students that they will participate in a group discussion using behaviors consistent with the roles they have been assigned. Members should not reveal their assigned roles to other group members.
4. Instruct groups to discuss the following question for about ten minutes: "Should prostitution be legalized?"
5. After the group discussion, ask members to guess which members were role playing task, maintenance, and self-centered roles.

TEACHING TIPS

This activity works well after the class has a basic understanding of functional theory. The activity can be repeated by varying the assigned roles. Another alternative is to role play only the self-centered roles, then role play only task and maintenance roles. Discussion questions:

- ❖ Were you able to guess the types of roles being performed by other group members?
- ❖ Which members made useful contributions to the group discussion?
- ❖ How do self-centered roles affect group interaction?
- ❖ Why is it important to have both task and maintenance roles represented in a group?
- ❖ In other group situations, do you usually find yourself following your assigned role or other ones? How did you react to having to play the assigned role?

FUNCTIONAL ROLES

TASK FUNCTIONS

INITIATOR
Proposes ideas and suggestions; provides direction for the group; gets the group started.

INFORMATION SEEKER
Asks for needed facts and figures; requests explanations and clarification of ideas; makes the group aware of information gaps.

INFORMATION GIVER
Provides the group with relevant information; researches, organizes, and presents needed information.

OPINION SEEKER
Asks for others' opinions; tests for group opinions and consensus; tries to discover what others believe or feel about an issue.

OPINION GIVER
States personal beliefs and interpretations; shares feelings; offers analysis and arguments.

CLARIFIER-SUMMARIZER
Explains ideas and their consequences; reduces confusion; sums up group progress and conclusions.

EVALUATOR-CRITIC
Assesses ideas, arguments, and suggestions; functions as the group's critical thinker; diagnoses task and procedural problems.

ENERGIZER
Motivates group members to do their best; helps create enthusiasm for the task and, if needed, a sense of urgency; serves as the group's "cheerleader."

PROCEDURAL TECHNICIAN
Assists with preparations for meetings including suggesting agenda items, making room arrangements, and providing needed materials and equipment.

RECORDER-SECRETARY
Keeps and provides accurate written records of a group's major ideas, suggestions, and decisions.

MAINTENANCE FUNCTIONS

ENCOURAGER-SUPPORTER
Praises and agrees with group members; provides recognition and person-to-person encouragement; listens empathetically.

HARMONIZER
Helps resolve conflicts; mediates differences among group members; emphasizes teamwork and the importance of everyone getting along.

COMPROMISER

Offers suggestions that minimize differences; helps the group reach consensus; searches for solutions acceptable to everyone.

TENSION RELEASER

Alleviates tension with friendly humor; breaks the ice and cools hot tempers; monitors tension levels and tries to relax the group.

GATEKEEPER

Monitors participation; encourages quiet members to speak and talkative members to stop; tries to control the flow of communication.

OBSERVER-INTERPRETER

Explains what others are trying to say; monitors and interprets feelings and nonverbal communication; expresses group feelings; paraphrases other members.

FOLLOWER

Supports the group and its members; accepts others' ideas and assignments; serves as an attentive audience member.

SELF-CENTERED FUNCTIONS

AGGRESSOR

Puts down members to get what he or she wants; sarcastic and critical of others; may take credit for someone else's work or idea.

BLOCKER

Stands in the way of progress; presents negative, disagreeable, and uncompromising positions; uses delaying tactics to derail an idea or proposal.

DOMINATOR

Prevents others from participating; asserts authority and tries to manipulate others; interrupts others and monopolizes discussion.

RECOGNITION SEEKER

Boasts about personal accomplishments; tries to impress others and become the center of attention; pouts or disrupts the discussion if not getting enough attention.

CLOWN

Injects inappropriate humor or commentary into the group; seems more interested in goofing off than working; distracts the group.

DESERTER

Withdraws from the group; appears "above it all" and annoyed or bored with the discussion; remains aloof or stops contributing.

CONFESSOR

Seeks emotional support from the group; shares very personal feelings and problems with members; uses the group for emotional support.

SPECIAL INTEREST PLEADER

Speaks on behalf of an outside group or a personal interest; tries to influence group members to support non-group interests.

CHAPTER 3

PARTICIPATION IN GROUPS

THE BEST GROUP FOR THE JOB

GOAL

- To discover how different members in a group can make valuable contributions toward a group's goal.

PARTICIPANTS

Groups of 5 to 7 members.

PROCEDURE

1. Distribute the *STARS Program* handout.
2. Instruct each group to identify any skills, resources, experiences, and personal qualities that members possess that would make them qualified to be appointed to STARS. Groups may not create fictional qualifications.
3. A spokesperson from each group will then explain to the class why his or her group is the best group for this job.
4. The class can then vote on the group that best meets the job requirements (other than his or her own group).

TEACHING TIPS

Encourage groups to think creatively when identifying individual members' potential contributions to the STARS goal. Offering the winning group extra credit may motivate students and generate enthusiasm for the activity. Discussion questions:

- ❖ Which group is "the best for the job?" Why?
- ❖ Did the best group have any weak areas?
- ❖ Why and how did you believe those weaknesses could be compensated for?
- ❖ Would the best group for this job be the best group for any job?
- ❖ How difficult was it to determine how each member could make a contribution?
- ❖ The textbook claims that the ideal group member must be ready, willing, and able to work with the group. Would the STARS group be able to accomplish its goal if any one of these requirements were missing?

STARS PROGRAM

STUDENTS ACTIVE IN RECRUITING STUDENTS

The college is seeking a group of students to develop a new program (STARS) to assist with recruitment. The college hopes that the STARS program will be a creative way to reach out to potential students. Members of the STARS group will be provided with full tuition, given priority during class registration, and paid a reasonable hourly wage for their work.

STARS will be responsible for a variety of tasks including the following: hosting an annual on-campus recruitment party, developing and maintaining a web site, writing an informational pamphlet, adhering to a budget, conducting tours of the campus, visiting local high schools, and assisting in the hiring of additional college recruiters.

The ideal group will consist of members who are creative thinkers, hard workers, knowledgeable of college services, enthusiastic, cooperative, and can respond to the various concerns of potential new students.

CHAPTER 3

PARTICIPATION IN GROUPS

MYERS-BRIGGS® TYPES: VIVE LA DIFFERENCE!

GOALS

- To demonstrate the differences between Myers-Briggs'® thinkers and feelers.
- To appreciate the value of different types in groups.
- To reinforce the need to adapt to members' work styles and preferences.

PARTICIPANTS

Groups of 5 to 7 members.

PROCEDURE

Instruct class members to list the key characteristics of an ideal professor/instructor. Divide the class into separate groups of thinkers and feelers based on their own assessment of Myers-Briggs® categories or their results on the MBTI.

1. Tell group members to share their individual lists with one another and produce a list of ten characteristics that describe an ideal college instructor.
2. A person from each group should write the group's list of characteristics on the board or a flip chart.
3. Lead the class in a discussion of the differences between the lists produced by thinking and feeling groups.

TEACHING TIPS

In addition to helping the class understand the differences between thinkers and feelers, this exercise can also demonstrate differences in the ways that thinkers and feelers work in groups. Thinkers often have a hard time *not* debating the virtues of their individual lists. They analyze the final result and may argue about order. Feelers may have a more sociable discussion. They are pleased to discover similarities on individual lists and may tell stories about their favorite teachers. A discussion of the group process may be just as important as a comparison of the final lists. In general, thinkers will focus on the instructor's intelligence and knowledge as well as how well he or she is organized. Not surprisingly, feelers will describe an ideal instructor as someone who cares about them, who makes students feel comfortable and appreciated. Discussion questions:

- ❖ What, if any, are the common characteristics?
- ❖ How do thinkers and feelers view the ideal professor/instructor?
- ❖ How can teachers use this information to improve instruction?

CHAPTER 3
PARTICIPATION IN GROUPS

TALKING TOKENS

GOALS

- To demonstrate the differences between Myers-Briggs® extroverts and introverts.
- To reinforce the need to adapt to members' work styles and preferences.
- To encourage extroverts to let introverts contribute in their own way and time.

PARTICIPANTS

A group of 6 to 8 members.

PROCEDURE

1. Select 3 or 4 students who are clearly extroverts and 3 or 4 who are clearly introverts. Put them in a single group but make sure there are equal numbers of extroverts and introverts.
2. Give each group member three "talking tokens" (e.g., slips of paper, coins, marbles, paper clips). Each time a participant talks, he or she must put a "talking token" on the table. When all of a person's tokens are gone, he or she cannot talk again until everyone has used up all of their tokens.
3. Choose a controversial topic about which everyone should have an opinion. The topic can be a national news story, a local community issue, or a campus controversy. Tell the group to discuss the topic until they're told to stop.
4. Tell the rest of the class to observe.
5. After about 15 minutes, stop the exercise and begin the discussion.

TEACHING TIPS

This exercise can provide a dramatic demonstration of the differences between extroverts and introverts. You may have to intervene at various times to remind the group of the rules. Extroverts will often keep talking even when they have used up all their tokens. Introverts often find this exercise frustrating because they have trouble getting started and are often interrupted by extroverts who throw their own token on the table. You may have to stop the exercise before it is completed because everyone is so frustrated. Discussion questions:

- ❖ Who ran out of "talking tokens" first?
- ❖ How did they react when they ran out?
- ❖ Did some members run out before others had used their first token?
- ❖ Did the introverts look comfortable during the discussion? Why or why not?
- ❖ Did the extroverts look frustrated? How do you know?
- ❖ Who talked the longest? Who talked the least? Was there a difference in the substance or value of what members said?
- ❖ How would you describe the group climate, from beginning to end?

CHAPTER 4

CONFIDENCE IN GROUPS

SORTING THE SYMPTOMS

GOAL

- To summarize and understand the symptoms of communication apprehension.

PARTICIPANTS

Groups of 5 to 7 members.

PROCEDURE

This exercise is provided in the Groupwork section of the chapter.

1. Instruct students to make a list of the symptoms of communication apprehension (increased heart rate, excessive perspiration, filler phrases such as "you know" and "OK") that they have experienced when speaking to a group or giving a public presentation.
2. Create a master list of symptoms by combining the lists of all group members.
3. Identify the symptoms that are more likely to occur during a group discussion.

TEACHING TIPS

The activity works well as an introduction to communication apprehension. After talking about the symptoms with other group members, students begin to realize that their fears are normal and often experienced by others. Discussion questions:

- ❖ How can the type of group or topic of discussion affect the number and severity of communication apprehension symptoms?
- ❖ Which symptoms can or cannot be seen or heard by other group members?
- ❖ Does knowing that some of the symptoms are not apparent to others reduce any of the “meta-anxiety” (anxiety about anxiety) you may be experiencing?
- ❖ What is the relationship, if any, between the number and type of symptoms and a person's PRCA score for groups, meetings, interpersonal communication, and public speaking?
- ❖ How can you alleviate some of the causes and symptoms of communication apprehension in groups?

CHAPTER 4

CONFIDENCE IN GROUPS

COGNITIVE RESTRUCTURING

GOALS

- To identify irrational thoughts and sources of communication apprehension associated with working in groups.
- To develop strategies for minimizing group members' communication apprehension.

PARTICIPANTS

After students work individually, the class divides into groups of 3 to 4 members.

PROCEDURE

1. Distribute copies of the *Cognitive Restructuring* worksheet.
2. Ask students to answer the following questions: What group situations make you most nervous? What are you most afraid will happen to you during a group discussion?
3. Instruct students to identify in the first column of the worksheet at least three of their worst fears related to working in groups. For example, "I am afraid that the group won't take my ideas seriously."
4. Divide the class into groups of 3 to 4 members.
5. Instruct the groups to develop a prevention strategy for minimizing the risk of each group member's fears. For example, "I will carefully think through my idea and speak confidently when I speak to the group."
6. Instruct students to create positive statements to replace their negative thoughts of working in groups. For example, "I have a good idea that will be appreciated by the group when they hear it," or "The group's rejection of my suggestion doesn't mean that they dislike me and my ideas."

TEACHING TIPS

Cognitive restructuring assumes that eliminating irrational and negative thoughts can reduce communication apprehension. In addition, it encourages students to confront their fears and replace them with more positive thoughts. Follow the activity with a class discussion of their fears and responses. Consider having students complete the *Personal Report of Communication Apprehension* (PRCA24) at the end of Chapter 4 before conducting this activity. Discussion questions:

- ❖ What did you find helpful about the exercises? What, if anything, did you not find helpful?
- ❖ Can you identify groups you participate in where you can apply the prevention strategies?

COGNITIVE RESTRUCTURING

FEAR	PREVENTION STRATEGY	POSITIVE SELF-TALK

CHAPTER 4

CONFIDENCE IN GROUPS

SYSTEMATIC DESENSITIZATION

GOALS

- To learn a deep muscle relaxation technique as a means of relieving the level of communication apprehension.
- To help students visualize a series of positive group communication situations.

PARTICIPANTS

Entire class.

PROCEDURE

1. Instruct students to make themselves as physically comfortable as possible in their seats or on the floor.
2. Inform students that they will be tensing and relaxing the different muscle groups of the body. The basic procedure is as follows:
   - Tense the muscle for 5 to 10 seconds.
   - Release the tension. Relax the muscle by letting it go as limp as possible.
3. Begin leading students through the relaxation exercises. Follow the sequence and directions listed in the *Muscle Relaxation* handout.
4. After all muscle groups have been relaxed, ask students to visualize a series of group communication situations. Examples of situations are listed in the *Group Communication Hierarchy.* Each situation should be visualized for 5 to 10 seconds. Between each visualization, remind students to continue to relax.

TEACHING TIPS

When conducting this activity, consider playing calm instrumental music in the background. Several practice sessions are normally necessary for most students to effectively learn a relaxation technique. Distribute copies of the *Muscle Relaxation* handout and suggest that students continue practicing on their own. Follow the session with a class discussion. Discussion questions:

- ❖ Did you feel the difference between tensing and relaxing your muscles? Were some muscle groups more difficult to relax than others?
- ❖ Which visualizations created the most anxiety?
- ❖ Were you able to remain relaxed throughout the visualizations?

MUSCLE RELAXATION

MUSCLE GROUPS	INSTRUCTIONS
Left hand and arm	Make a fist.
Right hand and arm	Make a fist.
Both hands and arms	Clench hands into fists.
Shoulders	Shrug your shoulders.
Forehead and brow	Raise eyebrows and wrinkle nose.
Eyes and face	Squeeze eyes tightly.
Jaws and face	Smile and clench teeth tightly.
Neck	Lean head slightly back, then pull head slightly forward.
Chest	Breathe deeply and hold.
Stomach	Make abdomen tight and hard.
Right leg	Point toes away from you, then point them toward you.
Left leg	Point toes away from you, then point them toward you.

GROUP COMMUNICATION HIERARCHY

1. You are having a casual conversation with a group member before a meeting.
2. Your group is scheduled to meet tomorrow and you have not had time to prepare.
3. You are introducing yourself to a group in which you are the only new member.
4. Group members are taking turns presenting their opinions on an issue. Your turn is next.
5. You are trying to make a point in a group discussion when you feel that everyone is looking at you.
6. Another group member has just asked you a difficult question.
7. The group's leader has unexpectedly called on you to present some information.
8. You have raised a controversial issue and group members have begun arguing.
9. You have been appointed the chairperson of the meeting.
10. You are a member of a group doing a panel presentation for a large audience.

CHAPTER 4

CONFIDENCE IN GROUPS

I DON'T MEAN TO BRAG BUT. . .

GOAL

- To allow students an additional opportunity to gain experience speaking in front of a group.
- To allow students the opportunity to convey positive attributes about themselves.

PARTICIPANTS

Entire class

PROCEDURE

1. The class period prior to the intended presentations, assign students a 1 to 2 minute speech. Inform them that they will not be graded on the speech; you will simply check off their names as having completed the assignment.
2. The subject of the speech is to be "An accomplishment I am proud of." Point out that the accomplishments may come in any number of areas, such as having raised a family successfully, won a letter in a high school sport, learned to play an instrument, opened a business, etc.
3. On the day of the speeches, encourage the students to ask one another questions about their accomplishments.

TEACHING TIPS

While students generally like to talk about themselves, many are reluctant to brag—unless they are required to do so. This assignment allows students to have a positive speaking experience. It also allows students to find out about what others in the group have accomplished. Discussion questions:

- ❖ How did you feel about having to share something positive about yourself?
- ❖ Did others list accomplishments that surprised you?
- ❖ Did you find individuals with whom you share an accomplishment?
- ❖ How can you use this information to facilitate group communication?

CHAPTER 5

VERBAL AND NONVERBAL COMMUNICATION IN GROUPS

CONTEXT, CONTEXT, CONTEXT

GOAL

- To demonstrate the extent to which the meanings of language and nonverbal behavior are dependent on social climate and group circumstances.

PARTICIPANTS

Groups of at least 3 members.

PROCEDURE

This exercise is provided in the Groupwork section of the chapter.

1. Each group creates a situation in which the following sentence is uttered: "I don't think that's right." The group must:
   - Decide what sentence came before and after, "I don't think that's right."
   - Decide upon the physical setting and situation confronting the group in which a member would say, "I don't think that's right."
2. Each group creates a "scene" in which three different group members are assigned to "act" the three sentences they have developed and placed in a specific context.
3. The groups should "perform" their scenes for the class.

TEACHING TIPS

The activity works best after students are familiar with the textbook material on both verbal and nonverbal communication. The class should discuss the following questions:

- ❖ How did the context or situation change the meaning of "I don't think that's right?"
- ❖ How did the nonverbal behavior and setting differ in each scene?
- ❖ How could each group's "I don't think that's right" be paraphrased into a different sentence?
- ❖ Which component communicated the most information about the meaning of the scene—the words, the nonverbal behavior, or the situation?

CHAPTER 5

VERBAL AND NONVERBAL COMMUNICATION IN GROUPS

SPACE INVASION

GOAL

- To demonstrate the different zones of interaction identified by Edward T. Hall.

PARTICIPANTS

The entire class divided into 2 large groups.

PROCEDURE

1. Divide the class into two large groups. If there is an uneven number of participants, the instructor should join the smaller group.
2. The first group should form a line against the wall at the front of the room.
3. The second group should form a straight line facing the first group. The groups should be at least eight feet apart. Any furniture in the space between the two lines must be moved out of the way.
4. Have each group identify a partner from the opposite line directly facing them. If necessary, have the groups adjust the line to make sure each person is lined up with his or her partner in the opposite group.
5. Identify the center between the two groups. Instruct them to do the following:
   - Walk toward your partner in the other group and meet in the center. Stand nose to nose with that person without actually touching him or her.
   - When the instructor tells you to do so, step back to a distance that would be comfortable for holding a casual conversation with this person.
   - Instruct students to extend their arms to determine the approximate distance at which they are standing.

TEACHING TIPS

This activity is a quick and effective way to demonstrate Hall's four zones of interaction. Another way to form the groups is to tell students to choose a partner who is about the same height and then stand in opposite lines from that person. If your classroom is small, this activity can be conducted easily in a wide hallway. The activity should be followed by a discussion of distance and group interaction. Discussion questions:

- ❖ What was the distance between partners when the lines were first formed?
- ❖ What was distance between partners when you stood nose to nose? Was this uncomfortable? Why?
- ❖ What was the distance when you were about an arm's length away from your partner?
- ❖ At what distances do you think most members interact when working in groups?
- ❖ How does culture or gender influence the use of distance during group interaction?

CHAPTER 5

VERBAL AND NONVERBAL COMMUNICATION IN GROUPS

HOW OFTEN IS OFTEN?

GOALS

- To demonstrate that meanings are determined by people, not words.
- To illustrate the problems associated with using abstract language.

PARTICIPANTS

Groups of 4 to 6 members.

PROCEDURE

1. Distribute copies of the *How Often Is Often?* handout to the class.
2. Review with the class the instructions contained in the handout for the activity. In addition, emphasize the following guidelines:
   - There are no right or wrong answers to the items.
   - Assign each item a number based on what you believe may be accurate.
   - Work quickly, writing down the first answer that comes to mind.
3. After everyone has completed the handout, divide the class into groups.
4. Group members should compare their answers for all items.

TEACHING TIPS

Initially, some students may be confused about assigning a numerical value to the words. It may be helpful to instruct students to think in terms of percentages. For example, assigning 10 to "hardly ever" would represent that "hardly ever" has a ten percent likelihood of occurring. This activity should be followed with a discussion of the sources of meanings for words and the importance of using concrete words.
Discussion questions:

- ❖ How similar or dissimilar were your answers compared to other group members?
- ❖ How precise do you think these words are in describing frequencies and quantities?
- ❖ What kinds of problems can be created in work groups when using abstract or imprecise language?
- ❖ Would the activity have been easier if contexts for the words had been provided?

HOW OFTEN IS OFTEN?

PART I: FREQUENCY

Instructions: The following words are commonly used to represent the frequency of events. For each word or phrase, specify a number between 0 and 100 to indicate how many times an event has occurred or is likely to occur. For example, if "hardly ever" means to you that something occurs 10 percent of the time, place a 10 in the blank space by that item.

______	1.	often	______	6.	usually
______	2.	never	______	7.	almost always
______	3.	always	______	8.	rarely
______	4.	frequently	______	9.	not often
______	5.	sometimes	______	10.	hardly ever

PART II: QUANTITY

Instructions: The following words are commonly used to represent quantities. For each word or phrase, specify the number you think most accurately represents that term. In other words, how many is "a few?"

______ 1. a few
______ 2. a lot
______ 3. several
______ 4. many
______ 5. some

CHAPTER 5

VERBAL AND NONVERBAL COMMUNICATION IN GROUPS

PLEASE BE SEATED

GOAL

- To understand the effect seating arrangements have on group interaction.

PARTICIPANTS

Groups of 5 to 7 members.

PROCEDURE

1. Instruct the groups that they are responsible for arranging the classroom in preparation for a meeting of 12 group members.
2. The groups should first decide on an arrangement using the classroom furniture that would promote interaction.
3. Groups should then develop an arrangement that would discourage interaction within a group.
4. A spokesperson for each group should explain the two arrangements to the class.

TEACHING TIPS

Depending on the constraints of your classroom, the student spokesperson may explain the group's arrangement, draw it on the board, or actually rearrange the furniture in the classroom. A variation of this activity has groups develop different arrangements that also reflect a particular type of leadership. Discussion questions:

- ❖ In what ways would the groups' first arrangements encourage interaction?
- ❖ In what ways do the groups' second arrangements discourage interaction?
- ❖ If you could choose any place on your campus other than your classroom for a meeting, where would you choose to meet? Why?
- ❖ Would you be able to create arrangements that better promoted interaction if you had different furniture available? If so, in what ways would interaction improve?

CHAPTER 5

VERBAL AND NONVERBAL COMMUNICATION IN GROUPS

ONE SYLLABLE TALK: AN INTERCULTURAL EXPERIENCE

GOAL

- To experience the challenge of speaking with a limited language ability.
- To empathize with those who have limited language skills.
- To demonstrate how vocabulary and language facility affects communication.

PARTICIPANTS

Groups of 5 to 7 members.

PROCEDURE

1. Assign a discussion topic or simple problem-solving exercise to groups consisting of 5 to 7 members.
2. Group members may only speak using one-syllable words.
3. After the group discussions, reassemble the class and discuss the difficulties and frustrations of communicating with limited language ability.

TEACHING TIPS

This exercise is an efficient way of demonstrating how vocabulary and language ability affect communication efficiency and effectiveness. Students will discover that their thinking must be divided into two parts. One part of their thinking focuses on the topic and progress of the discussion. The other part of their thinking focuses on finding the best one-syllable words to express their ideas and opinions. For many students, this exercise dramatizes the challenges faced by non-native speakers of English and adults with speech disabilities. Discussion questions:

- ❖ What ideas and opinions were most difficult to express?
- ❖ How did the one-syllable rule affect your thinking process?
- ❖ How would you describe the speaking style used by group members during the discussion?
- ❖ What were your biggest frustrations during this exercise?
- ❖ How did the one-syllable rule affect the outcome of the discussion/speech?

ALTERNATIVE FORMS OF THE ONE-SYLLABLE TALK EXERCISE:

1. Require half the group to speak in one-syllable words and the other half to speak normally. The inequities, frustrations, and divisions between the two groups will emerge.
2. Ask students to give a 60-second impromptu speech using only one-syllable words. The entire class can be asked to speak on the same topic or can select an impromptu topic from an envelope right before they speak. Examples of topics: My career goals; My favorite pastime; My unique family; My pet.

CHAPTER 5

VERBAL AND NONVERBAL COMMUNICATION IN GROUPS

NAME THAT EMOTION

GOALS

- To demonstrate that emotions are observable, public behaviors.
- To identify the most universally recognized emotions.
- To illustrate how we express emotions nonverbally.

PARTICIPANTS

Entire class

PROCEDURE

1. Select a volunteer willing to and capable of demonstrating emotions through facial expressions.
2. Ask the student to sit in a chair facing the class. Give the student nine cards with the name of a single emotion on each card. Emotions: anger, sadness, happiness, fear, surprise, disgust, contempt, love, hope.
3. Tell the volunteer to make the appropriate facial expression for each emotion.
4. Ask the class to guess and write down the emotions they can identify.
5. Count and compare the percent of successful guesses with each emotion.

TEACHING TIPS

This activity helps demonstrate that emotions are behavioral, public, and amenable to scientific study. It also allows opportunities to discuss both the pervasiveness of nonverbal communication and potential attendant problems. Discussion questions:

- ❖ Which emotions were easiest and most difficult to identify?
- ❖ If there were misperceptions, what caused them?
- ❖ Are these emotional expressions universal across cultures?
- ❖ Can individuals manipulate their nonverbal behaviors?

Variation: Videotape a male and female student demonstrating the list of emotions. Select volunteers with acting talent or highly expressive faces. Make sure you get a release from the volunteers so you can show the videotape to classes. There are several advantages to using videotape. You can be sure that the emotions will be well expressed. Also, because the rest of class will not know the volunteers, their facial expressions will not be compromised by personal familiarity. Videotaping a male and female allows you to use the most appropriate tape for a particular class or to contrast the ways in which men and women express emotions. As you videotape, review each emotion to make sure the student's facial expression is typical of that emotion. If not, retape the emotion.

CHAPTER 5

VERBAL AND NONVERBAL COMMUNICATION IN GROUPS

TEACHER, YOU MADE A MISTAKE

GOALS

- To make students more aware of problems in communication delivery

PARTICIPANTS

Entire class

PROCEDURE

1. Begin the class session on your normal course material by exhibiting several of the most common mistakes that presenters make. You might do things such as come late to class, be unorganized, speak in a monotone, maintain poor eye contact, lack sufficient handouts, etc.
2. After about 10 minutes, resume your normal style of teaching.
3. Ask the class to identify the poor communicative behaviors that you were exhibiting.

TEACHING TIPS

For many students, seeing the problems is more compelling than having you just talk about them. Having students focus on the instructor's mistakes rather than those of students can reduce apprehension concerns. Discussion questions:

- ❖ Were any of you uncomfortable during the exercise? What thoughts were going through your mind?
- ❖ How would you have reacted if this had lasted an entire class session?
- ❖ Did these behaviors have any impact on your judgment of my credibility?
- ❖ Have you seen other speakers make any of these mistakes? How did it affect your judgments of them?
- ❖ What can you do to avoid making these mistakes?

CHAPTER 5

VERBAL AND NONVERBAL COMMUNICATION IN GROUPS

EVERYONE KNOWS WHAT I MEAN

GOALS

- To illustrate the difficulties of interpreting meaning when ambiguous language is used.
- To allow students to see how their backgrounds may have an impact on the interpretation of words.

PARTICIPANTS

Entire class

PROCEDURE

1. Distribute copies of the *Everyone Knows What I Mean* handout.
2. Have students write down their answers quickly, putting down the first answer that comes to mind.
3. After the students have completed the handout, go through each question with the class, finding the high and low range for each question. It may help to write the range on the board.

TEACHING TIPS

This exercise allows discussion about the imprecision of commonly used language. It also allows opportunities for discussion of how our individual backgrounds may affect our perceptions and linguistic choices. Discussion questions:

- ❖ How similar or dissimilar were your responses compared to the rest of the class?
- ❖ How precise do you think the words were in terms of frequency and quantity?
- ❖ Why did people have different responses?
- ❖ How much of our interpretation of the meaning of words in each of these areas can be traced to our own backgrounds and situations?
- ❖ Were there any responses that really surprised you?
- ❖ Did the gender of the person named make any difference in your responses? Were you alerted to questions of gender in answering the salary question?
- ❖ What kinds of problems can be created in work groups when using very abstract or imprecise language?

EVERYONE KNOWS WHAT I MEAN

1. Diego is middle-aged. How old is he?

2. Mary makes an excellent salary. How much per year does she make?

3. John is a heavy smoker. How much does he smoke in a day?

4. Mike has a very good grade point average. What is his G.P.A.?

5. Ky bought an expensive car. How much did it cost?

6. Linda has many friends. How many friends does she have?

7. Suyan applied to several colleges. How many colleges did she apply to?

8. Hong reads quite a few books each year. How many does he read?

9. Leticia wants the project report on her desk soon. When does she want it?

10. Bob makes an excellent salary. How much per year does he make?

CHAPTER 6

LISTENING IN GROUPS

HOLD YOUR TONGUE AND LISTEN

GOALS

- To demonstrate how difficult it can be "hold your tongue" while listening.
- To demonstrate the value of comprehensive and analytic listening for discerning discussion problems related to inadequate information or misinformation.
- To listen empathically to misinformed and/or frustrated group members.
- To listen comprehensively, analytically, and appreciatively to well-informed group members.

PARTICIPANTS

Groups of 4 members

PROCEDURE

1. Ask every student to write down three subjects on which they consider themselves to be well-informed, highly skilled, and/or experts: playing a particular sport, speaking a second language, raising children, providing good customer service, repairing a car, oil painting, braiding hair, dancing, etc.
2. Divide the class into groups of four.
3. Each group member should select one of his or her "expert" topics and ask the other group members to discuss that topic for 4 to 8 minutes. The person whose topic is being discussed may not speak at all for the first half of the discussion. At the halfway point, the instructor will signal that the "expert" may join the discussion.
4. Every group member's topic should be discussed during the exercise.

TEACHING TIPS

This group exercise can demonstrate all four types of listening. The "expert" must listen comprehensively and analytically to other group members during the first half of the discussion in order to note incorrect information and/or opinions. When the "expert" rejoins the discussion, group members should engage in comprehensive and analytical listening in order to correct their misperceptions or factual errors. The "expert" must listen empathically in order to maintain emotional control, particularly if a group is "getting it all wrong." When the "expert" rejoins the group and adds authoritative information and opinions, group members should also listen appreciatively. Discussion questions:

❖ How did you feel when listening to group members discuss your topic, particularly when their facts or opinions were incorrect?
❖ How did you feel when listening to the "expert" who rejoined the group's discussion at the halfway point?
❖ What emotions did you feel during this discussion? Did these emotions affect the way you listened?

CHAPTER 6

LISTENING IN GROUPS

FOUR SQUARES

GOALS

- To demonstrate the importance of effective listening in groups.
- To demonstrate listening behaviors necessary to comprehend information.

PARTICIPANTS

Groups of 6 to 8 members.

PROCEDURE

1. Divide the class into groups. Appoint one member of each group to be a presenter.
2. Provide each presenter with a copy of *Four Squares: Diagram 1*. The presenters are not to show the diagram to the other group members.
3. Instruct the presenters to briefly describe the diagram to the group by following these guidelines:
   - Group members should only listen.
   - Presenters should not use hand gestures during their descriptions.
   - Students may not ask questions of the presenter or make comments to each other.
4. Tell the listeners in the groups to draw the diagram on a sheet of paper as described by the presenter.
5. Distribute to the presenters a copy of *Four Squares: Diagram 2*. Inform the groups that:
   - This time they know they will be asked to redraw a diagram based on the presenter's descriptions.
   - The listeners may ask as many questions of the presenter as necessary to accurately redraw the diagram.
   - The presenter may describe the diagram in any way, except by actually drawing it for the group or revealing the handout.
6. After the second drawing has been completed, let the presenter share a copy of the diagram with the group.

TEACHING TIPS

This activity works best when students do not know that they will be asked to redraw the first diagram based on the presenter's description. Consider asking students how accurate their first drawings are before moving on to the second part of the activity. Discussion questions:

- ❖ Why wasn't your first drawing very accurate? Why was the second drawing more accurate?
- ❖ Did listener feedback improve the presenter's subsequent descriptions? Did a group member's question significantly help other members complete the task successfully?

FOUR SQUARES: DIAGRAM 1

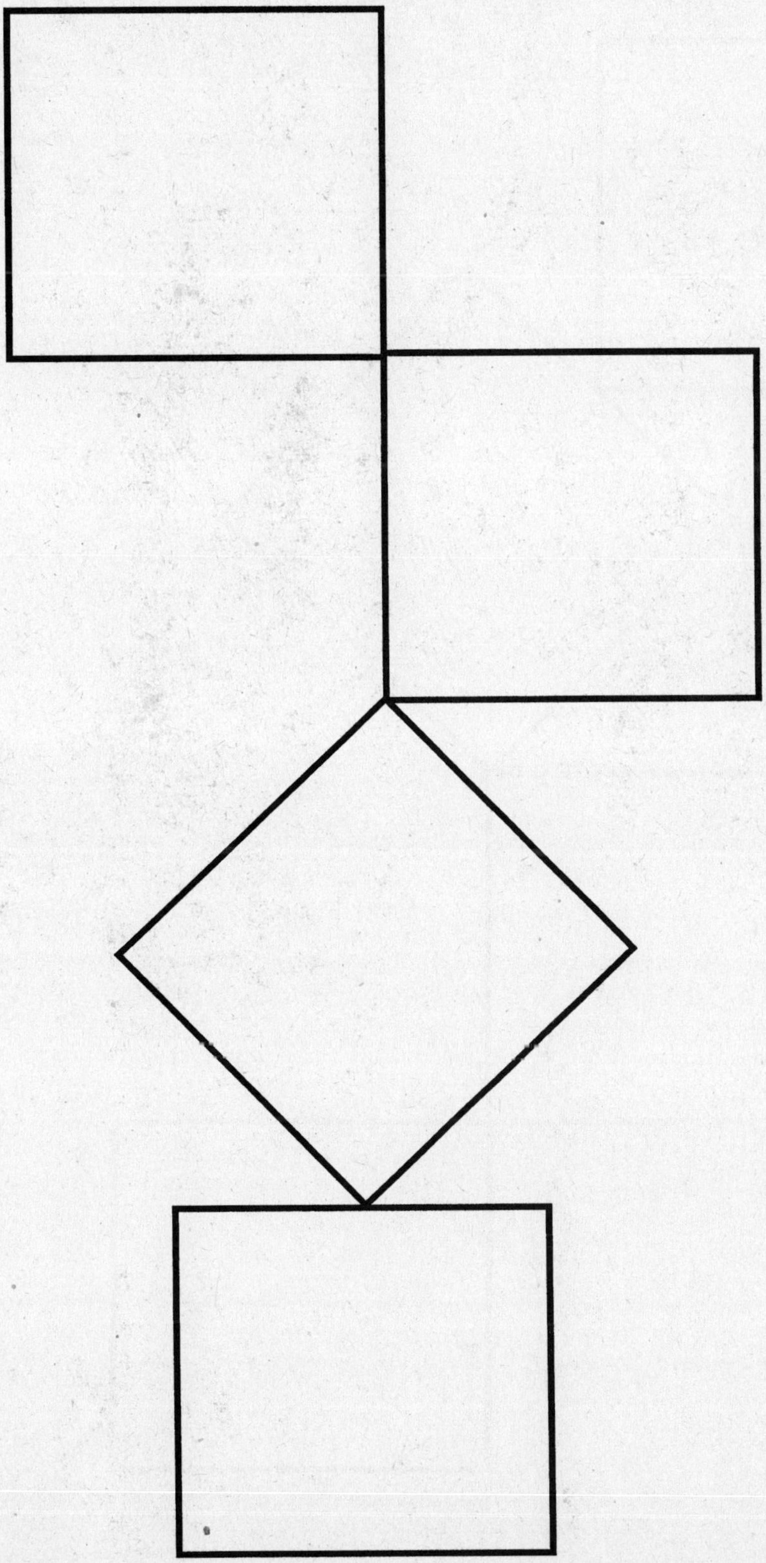

FOUR SQUARES: DIAGRAM 2

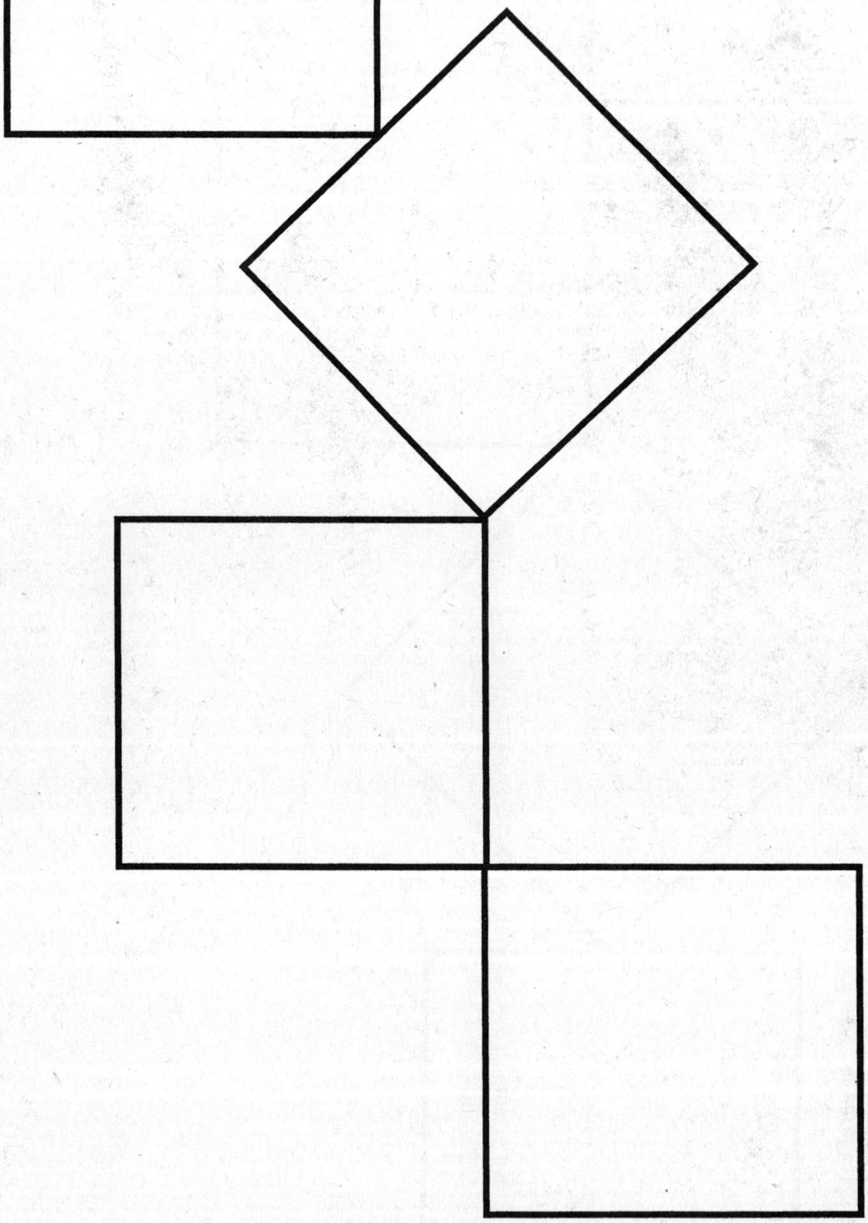

CHAPTER 6

LISTENING IN GROUPS

ARE YOU LISTENING?

GOALS

- To demonstrate the importance of listening.
- To demonstrate that most of us are inefficient listeners.

PARTICIPANTS

Entire class.

PROCEDURE

1. Before class, select two or three paragraphs from a magazine, newspaper, or journal article. Try to choose material that students are unlikely to find interesting.
2. Do not introduce the activity. Simply begin reading the article.
3. After finishing, tell the group to write down five things they remember from the article.

TEACHING TIPS

You may wish to modify the activity by asking students specific questions about the article. Another option is to read a second article instructing them to listen carefully and take notes. The class can then compare listening efficiency between the two readings. Follow the activity with a discussion of strategies to improve listening. Discussion questions:

- ❖ Did the failure to provide a context for the exercise have any impact on your listening skills? What can you conclude from that?
- ❖ Why was the class able to recall so few details from the article?
- ❖ What are the potential consequences of poor listening in groups?
- ❖ What could you have done to improve your listening during this activity?

CHAPTER 6

LISTENING IN GROUPS

LISTENING TRIADS

GOAL

- To give group members an opportunity to understand their listening strengths and weaknesses.

PARTICIPANTS

Groups of 3 members.

PROCEDURE

1. Before beginning the exercise, all group members should complete Shafir's Self-Listening Test assessment instrument included at the end of Chapter 6 of the textbook.
2. There are three rounds in the Listening Triads exercise. Each round includes three tasks:
   - The speaker selects and explains two or three items from the instrument that best describe his or her listening strengths and/or weaknesses.
   - The listener listens and may ask questions to help the speaker explain why certain skills are strengths or weaknesses. The listener summarizes the speaker's main ideas.
   - The observer observes the listener and provides feedback about the listener's listening behavior and summary.
3. Triads have five minutes for each round of listening. After each round is completed, the group should discuss the listening behavior of the listener.
4. At the end of three rounds, the group should discuss what they learned or observed from the exercise.

TEACHING TIPS

This activity can be conducted either as an introduction to a listening unit or following instruction of strategies for improving listening. Discussion questions:

❖ What general observations can we make about our listening behavior? How easy or difficult was the exercise for the listener?

❖ How can we improve our listening behavior?

CHAPTER 6

LISTENING IN GROUPS

DIFFERENT NOTES FOR DIFFERENT FOLKS

GOAL

- To understand how members' listening skills may differ.
- To discover different methods of taking notes.
- To discover the advantages of group listening.

PARTICIPANTS

Groups of 5 to 7 members.

PROCEDURE

1. Have students view an instructional film of your choosing in class.
2. Instruct all students to take notes as they view the film. Informing students that they will be tested on the material may provide motivation for good note taking.
3. After viewing the film, instruct students to get in groups to compare notes. Students should look for similarities and differences in the content and style of their notes.

TEACHING TIPS

Any instructional film can be used for this activity. Choosing a film that addresses issues directly relevant to the content of a small group communication course allows for an efficient use of classroom time by combining a useful film with an activity. If such films are not available to you, look to your college's library for films that focus on skills for student success. Choosing a film from a different discipline, e.g. biology or history, can make the activity more challenging. Discussion questions:

- ❖ Did different group members note different information?
- ❖ Did any group member have a complete set of notes?
- ❖ How effectively do you think you listened to the film?
- ❖ What types of listening did you use while listening to the film?
- ❖ Did other members use methods of taking notes that might be helpful to you? What were they? How will you plan on using them?
- ❖ What are the advantages of group listening over individual listening?

CHAPTER 6

LISTENING IN GROUPS

LISTENING EXCUSES, EXCUSES, EXCUSES

GOALS

- To identify the many reasons why people don't listen well.
- To suggest ways of overcoming poor listening habits.

PARTICIPANTS

Entire class.

PROCEDURE

1. Ask class members to think about and write down some of the reasons why they do not listen effectively in a variety of situations and settings.
2. Ask class members to volunteer reasons why they do not listen well and post those reasons on a flip chart, board, transparencies, or computer projection.
3. After a long list has been posted, ask the class to identify the reasons that, in their opinions, are responsible for the most serious listening problems.
4. Begin a discussion of ways in which good listeners overcome some of these serious listening problems.

TEACHING TIPS

By letting class members generate individual lists before speaking, they will have something to add to the discussion rather than worrying about whether they will be called on to speak. Go around the room asking students to identify the reason they think is most responsible for poor listening. When students identify similar reasons, you may want to consolidate those reasons into a single item and note how many times that reason is identified. Keep going around the room until the class runs out of reasons. Star (☆) the most important reasons and ask the class to suggest ways to overcome the listening problem. If the class has difficulty beginning this exercise, offer some typical listening problems: boring topic; speaker with poor speaking skills; daydreaming; strongly disagree with the speaker; distracted by personal problem; tired. Discussion questions:

- ❖ Was it difficult or easy for you to generate a list?
- ❖ Did other students mention items you had not thought of?
- ❖ What can you do to overcome these problems?

CHAPTER 6

LISTENING IN GROUPS

LISTENING TO LEARN

GOALS

- To emphasize the importance of listening skills as a prerequisite for learning.
- To demonstrate the importance of using listening skills before, during, and after listening to messages in a classroom setting.
- To improve students' ability to listen and learn.

PARTICIPANTS

Groups of 5 to 6 members.

PROCEDURE

1. Ask students to complete the *Listening to Learn Survey*. Emphasize that the survey will ask them about their listening behavior before, during, and after they attend a class.
2. After each student has completed the survey, ask students to form groups and discuss the following questions:
    - Which listening behaviors do you do before, during, and after class?
    - To what extent do you and your group believe that these behaviors can improve your ability to learn?
    - Which listeners' behaviors were strongest and weakest among group members?
3. Ask a spokesperson from each group to report their conclusions to the rest of the class.

TEACHING TIPS

Many students believe that listening skills only apply to behavior that occurs while someone else is speaking. This exercise emphasizes that students can "prepare" to listen more effectively before they attend class and that they can remember what they've heard better after class by engaging in a variety of listening behaviors. Some students may argue that the "before" and "after" activities are not really listening behaviors. The best response is that highly effective speakers plan their presentations before they speak and analyze their speeches after they speak in order to understand whether they have achieved their purpose. Good listeners can and should do the same. Discussion questions:

❖ Did any of these suggested items surprise you?
❖ Are there any items you have found particularly useful in the past?
❖ Are there any items you plan to adopt in the future?

LEARNING TO LISTEN SURVEY[1]

Listening is a key to learning in college. The following questions test your listening behavior:

Before you attend a class do you:

Review your notes from the previous class or classes?
- ❑ Yes, consistently ❑ No, almost never ❑ Sometimes

Become apprehensive if you know the subject matter will be tough?
- ❑ Yes, consistently ❑ No, almost never ❑ Sometimes

Let your opinion of the instructor affect your ability to listen?
- ❑ Yes, consistently ❑ No, almost never ❑ Sometimes

Plan on sitting in the back row when you expect a lecture to be difficult?
- ❑ Yes, consistently ❑ No, almost never ❑ Sometimes

Identify your listening goals, that is, what you want to learn from the class?
- ❑ Yes, consistently ❑ No, almost never ❑ Sometimes

Prepare to take appropriate notes?
- ❑ Yes, consistently ❑ No, almost never ❑ Sometimes

While you are attending a class do you:

Make yourself listen even when the speaker is boring?
- ❑ Yes, consistently ❑ No, almost never ❑ Sometimes

Listen objectively even if you don't agree with or like what is being said?
- ❑ Yes, consistently ❑ No, almost never ❑ Sometimes

Adapt your note taking to the speaker's style and content?
- ❑ Yes, consistently ❑ No, almost never ❑ Sometimes

Ask questions if you don't understand or if you need clarification?
- ❑ Yes, consistently ❑ No, almost never ❑ Sometimes

Make eye contact with the instructor during a lecture or discussion?
- ❑ Yes, consistently ❑ No, almost never ❑ Sometimes

After you have attended a class do you:

Go over your notes after class?
- ❑ Yes, consistently ❑ No, almost never ❑ Sometimes

Look up new vocabulary or review the textbook in order to understand difficult concepts?
- ❑ Yes, consistently ❑ No, almost never ❑ Sometimes

Summarize the main points of a lecture at its completion?
- ❑ Yes, consistently ❑ No, almost never ❑ Sometimes

Do you think about how the information could be used, e.g., on a test, to write a paper?
- ❑ Yes, consistently ❑ No, almost never ❑ Sometimes

Remember what you liked or disliked about the speaker rather than the lecture?
- ❑ Yes, consistently ❑ No, almost never ❑ Sometimes

Add personal comments and open questions to your notes?
- ❑ Yes, consistently ❑ No, almost never ❑ Sometimes

---

[1] The Listen to Learn Survey is based on the following research and questionnaire: Imhof, M. (1998). "What makes a good listener? Listening behavior in instructional settings," *International Journal of Listening*, 12, 81–105.

CHAPTER 7

CONFLICT AND COHESION IN GROUPS

WIN AS MUCH AS YOU CAN

GOAL

- To demonstrate the consequences of competitive and cooperative conflict styles within the context of small group communication.

PARTICIPANTS

One or more groups of 8 divided into four dyads (two-person subgroups). If the class number requires it, place 3 people in a "dyad;" avoid having any member acting individually.

PROCEDURE

This exercise is provided in the Groupwork section of the chapter.

1. Distribute copies of the payoff chart and tally sheet to students. The charts also appear in the textbook.
2. There are ten rounds in this exercise. During each round the two people in each dyad will have to choose an "X" or a "Y." The "payoff" for each round is determined by the choices made by all the dyads in the eight-person group.
3. Explain the following three key rules:
   - Do not confer with other members of your group unless you are told to do so.
   - Both members of a dyad must agree upon a single choice for each round.
   - Make sure that the other members of your group do not know your dyad's choice until you are told to reveal it.
4. The dyads are to confer with their partners on every round. Before rounds 5, 8, and 10, the dyads can confer with the other dyads in the group to try to develop a more cooperative approach to the activity.
5. After the groups have completed all ten rounds, ask each dyad to announce to the class their total wins or losses.

TEACHING TIPS

The exercise works best if the instructor remains out of the activity, only calling out the rounds and keeping order. If asked any questions, simply repeat the title of the exercise. After the students announce their totals, inform them that if everyone had cooperated throughout the exercise, each dyad would have won $25 and each group, $100.
Discussion questions:

❖ Did anyone make any linguistic assumptions? Did "you" mean "you" as a dyad or "you" as a group? Would a different decision made early have resulted in a different strategy?

❖ Did "win" mean win money or the trust and respect of your colleagues? If you had defined it as the latter, would you have played the game differently?

❖ As the groups became more competitive, what were some behaviors that you observed?

- What happened when trust began to break down in the group?
- Considering that none of the dyads came close to winning the maximum available dollars, how successful were the winners?
- Did some of the dyads feel betrayed by other group members?
- What are the consequences of a competitive approach to conflict on the effectiveness of a group?

WIN AS MUCH AS YOU CAN

Payoff Chart

4 Xs:	Lose $1.00 each
3 Xs: 1 Y:	Win $1.00 each Lose $3.00 each
2 Xs: 2 Ys:	Win $2.00 each Lose $2.00 each
1 X: 3 Ys:	Win $3.00 each Lose $1.00 each
4 Ys:	Win $1.00 each

Tally Sheet

Round	Time Allowed	Confer With	Choice	$ Won	$ Lost	Balance
1	2 min.	partner				
2	1 min.	partner				
3	1 min.	partner				
4	1 min.	partner				
5*	3min + 1 min.	group partner				
6	1 min.	partner				
7	1 min.	partner				
8†	3 min. + 1 min.	group partner				
9	1 min.	partner				
10‡	3 min. + 1 min.	group partner				

*Payoff is multiplied by 3
†Payoff is multiplied by 5
‡Payoff is multiplied by 10

CHAPTER 7

CONFLICT AND COHESION IN GROUPS

MEET THE MEDIATOR

GOAL

- To observe and experience the process of mediation in conflict resolution.

PARTICIPANTS

Groups of 5 to 6 members.

PROCEDURE

1. Select one member of each group to function as a mediator. Remind the mediators that they are not to take sides in the dispute. Their role is to guide group members toward a negotiated settlement of their conflict.
2. Distribute a copy of the case study entitled *Noisy Neighbors*.
3. Assign the other group members the neighbor roles in the dispute described in the case. Two members should role play the elderly couple. Two or three should role play the young college students.
4. Using the mediation steps described in the textbook, the mediator should try to resolve the conflict between the neighbors.
5. After all groups have reached a solution, ask the mediators to present the outcomes to the entire class.

TEACHING TIPS

This activity works best after students are familiar with the process of mediation presented in the textbook. Some groups will reach a resolution faster than others will. Discussion questions:

- ❖ As mediators, was it difficult to remain neutral?
- ❖ What was the most frustrating part of being a mediator?
- ❖ What could the mediators have done differently to improve the session?
- ❖ Did some members engage in behavior that made mediation more difficult?
- ❖ In what kinds of conflict situations does mediation work best? When would mediation not be an effective method of resolving conflict?

CASE STUDY: NOISY NEIGHBORS

The Armstrongs are an elderly couple in their mid 70s living on the fifth floor of a large apartment building. They spend most of their time at home reading and watching television. Right below them on the fourth floor is a group of college students sharing an apartment.

The Armstrongs have complained that the students' noisy lifestyle is disturbing them. The Armstrongs accuse them of playing loud music, slamming the door when they arrive home in the middle of the night, and yelling at each other from different rooms.

None of the other neighbors have complained to management about the noise. The students deny that they are excessively noisy. In fact, the students have accused the Armstrongs of turning the volume on the television up too loud when the students are trying to study. The Armstrongs have also complained about noise from the previous tenants. Both parties have agreed to resolve their dispute through mediation.

CHAPTER 7

CONFLICT AND COHESION IN GROUPS

WHAT'S IN A NAME?

GOAL

- To provide students with an opportunity to create a group identity.
- To illustrate the importance of group cohesion.

PARTICIPANTS

Groups of 5 to 7 members.

PROCEDURE

1. Inform students that they are to develop a study group for the purpose of preparing for the next test.
2. Groups should first identify their goal(s).
3. After goals have been identified, instruct the students to select a simple name for the group. For example, "Top Testers."
4. The students should then create a slogan for the group using 12 words or less. For example, "Working in groups to achieve academic excellence."
5. Finally, each group should create a graphic logo to represent its goals, name, and/or slogan.
6. After the above tasks have been completed, a representative from each group should present its name, slogan, and logo to the class.

TEACHING TIPS

Encourage groups to use this activity as an opportunity to form a study group for the next test. This activity can also be used when groups are formed for a major class project. The activity should be followed by a discussion of the importance of cohesive work groups. Discussion questions:

- ❖ Which group had the best name? Why? Which group had the best slogan? Why? Which group had the best logo? Why?
- ❖ How do you feel about the group you worked with?
- ❖ Do you think it is valuable to spend group time to develop cohesion? Why or why not?
- ❖ What else could a group do to enhance cohesion?

CHAPTER 7

COHESION AND CONFLICT IN GROUPS

THEY NEVER ASK FOR DIRECTIONS

GOALS

- To increase awareness of gender stereotypes.
- To illustrate the power of cultural conditioning and stereotyping.

PARTICIPANTS

Two large groups, one comprised of males and the other females

PROCEDURE

1. After dividing the class into two groups based on gender, ask each group to reflect on negative stereotypes about members of the other gender. They should generate a list of those characteristics.
2. Participants should be told that the stereotypes do not have to reflect their own attitudes, only those they believe to be held by many people. Students should be encouraged to offer specific examples to illustrate their points.
3. Have a spokesperson from each group present the list of the 10 most common stereotypes generated by the group. Do not allow members of the other group to respond to the list of stereotypes.

TEACHING TIPS

Care should be taken to note that the stereotypes are general societal beliefs, not necessarily ones held by specific class members. Discussion can also be expanded to include a focus on the role of stereotypes with respect to age, race, nationality, etc. Discussion questions:

- Were there any similarities in the negative stereotypes held by the male and female groups of each other? Were there dramatic differences?
- Did the "targeted" group feel there were any stereotypes that they would view as accurate? Were there any they would view as inaccurate?
- How did the "targeted" group feel about being unable to respond to perceived inaccurate stereotypes?
- Could this exercise be done with positive stereotypes?
- What implications do these stereotypes have on group cohesion and/or conflict?

CHAPTER 7

CONFLICT AND COHESION IN GROUPS

YOU TOO?

GOALS

- To allow students to focus on commonalities among group members.
- To allow students to recognize that finding commonalities usually requires effort.

PARTICIPANTS

Entire class

PROCEDURE

1. Distribute the *"You Too?"* handout to the class.
2. Have the members find a partner quickly. When given the signal to begin, they should attempt to find as many things in common with the other individual as they can and write them in the column under the person's name.
3. After 2 to 3 minutes, call time and have the students find another partner and repeat the process.
4. After 2 to 3 minutes, call time again and have students repeat the process once more with a different partner.

TEACHING TIPS

Tell students to pair off with students in the class they do not already know well. Encourage them to interact with persons of another gender, race or nationality while doing the exercise. This exercise can also be used during the initial class meetings.
Discussion questions:

- ❖ Was it easy or difficult to seek out commonalities? Did it make a difference depending on the person you were partnered with?
- ❖ How often do we tend to seek out commonalities? How often do we tend to focus on differences?
- ❖ How many of you found more than 15 items in common?
- ❖ Did you find any commonalities that surprised you?
- ❖ How did you discover the areas of commonality?
- ❖ What implications does this exercise have for working in groups?

YOU TOO?

List the things you find in common with three other people in the class.

Name	Name	Name

CHAPTER 7

COHESION AND CONFLICT IN GROUPS

PLEASE DON'T SAY THAT

GOALS

- To make students aware of the impact of culturally inappropriate remarks and/or actions.
- To provide students with skills in responding to culturally inappropriate remarks and/or actions.

PARTICIPANTS

Groups of 6 to 8 member

PROCEDURE

1. Discuss with students the process that should be used when culturally inappropriate remarks and/or actions happen in your presence. A generally accepted five-step process involves avoiding labeling, describing the problematic behavior, describing your reaction, requesting that the behavior be discontinued, and noting the consequences of a failure to change.
2. You may wish to have a student volunteer to role play a scenario.
3. Divide the class into groups of 6 to 8 and then have students pair off with other students.
4. Each student should describe an incident in which he or she heard a hurtful comment (e.g., racist, sexist, homophobic, etc.).
5. The partner should attempt to use proper interrupting techniques to deal with the offensive behavior.
6. The group should discuss and/or critique the responses, noting what was effective and what was ineffective.

TEACHING TIPS

Individuals who themselves would never make hurtful remarks are often at a loss to know how to respond when others do. This exercise gives students an opportunity to both recognize what can be hurtful and to learn how to respond to such actions.
Discussion questions:

- ❖ How often do we encounter off-handed prejudicial remarks?
- ❖ Why do we have difficulty confronting others about them?
- ❖ What effect can such remarks have on group cohesion?
- ❖ When would you choose to confront prejudicial remarks made in your group? When would you ignore them?
- ❖ What would be the benefits of addressing prejudicial remarks?

CHAPTER 8

LEADERSHIP IN GROUPS

WANTED: A FEW GOOD LEADERS

GOAL

- To analyze and discuss different perspectives of effective leadership.

PARTICIPANTS

Groups of 3 to 7 members.

PROCEDURE

This exercise is provided in the Groupwork section of the chapter.

1. Each student should complete *The Least-Preferred Coworker Scale* at the end of Chapter 8.
2. After everyone has completed the scale, they should form groups based on similar individual results, e.g. relationship-motivated students should join the same groups and task-motivated students should join other groups.
3. Each group should then work to write a description of the desired characteristics, skills, and/or duties of a potential leader in the form of a want ad in the employment section of the newspaper. Each advertisement should begin with:

   WANTED: LEADER
   The ideal candidate for this job will . . .

4. Each group should write or post its job description for the entire class to see. A spokesperson from each group should present the group's advertisement to the class.

TEACHING TIPS

Task-motivated groups and relationship-motivated groups tend to generate job descriptions that reflect their results on *The Least-Preferred Coworker Scale.* At times the differences will be very obvious. However, often the preferences are subtly evident in the language each group uses to describe similar leadership characteristics appearing in the advertisements of groups with opposite preferences. Discussion questions:

- ❖ What are the similarities among the want ads?
- ❖ What are the differences among the want ads?
- ❖ Which leadership theories apply to each want ad?
- ❖ In what ways did group members' preferences for relationship-motivation or task-motivation affect the words they chose to include in each want ad?
- ❖ Who was the leader in each group?
- ❖ Did the group designate a leader or did one emerge?

CHAPTER 8

LEADERSHIP IN GROUPS

NATURAL BORN LEADERS

GOAL

- To identify the traits that students believe are essential for effective leadership.

PARTICIPANTS

Groups of 5 to 7 members. (This activity can also be conducted with an entire class.)

PROCEDURE

1. Ask students to think of examples of excellent leaders. They may define for themselves the areas of leadership. Ask them to think about the characteristics of those leaders.
2. Instruct the groups to brainstorm and record as many traits as possible that are essential for or characteristic of effective leadership.

TEACHING TIPS

It may be helpful to introduce the guidelines for brainstorming explained in Chapter 9 of the textbook. If possible, groups should record their answers on a chalkboard so they are easy to reference during the class discussion. Follow the brainstorming session with a class discussion of trait theory. Discussion questions:

- ❖ If someone possesses all of these traits, will he or she be an effective leader?
- ❖ Are there effective leaders who do not possess most of these traits?
- ❖ Are there some traits that are more important than others are?
- ❖ How many of these traits describe a leader's communication skills?
- ❖ How valid do you think trait theory is as a way of explaining or predicting effective group leadership?

CHAPTER 8

LEADERSHIP IN GROUPS

SELECT A LEADER

GOALS

- To compare different leadership theories.
- To discuss the differences between designated leaders and emergent leaders.

PARTICIPANTS

Groups of 5 to 7 members.

PROCEDURE

1. Divide the class into groups. Distribute the case study entitled *Desert Isle*. Give them a few minutes to read and think about the situation.
2. Instruct the group to select a leader from the individuals described in the case study. The group should carefully consider the situation and each potential leader's profile. The group should be prepared to explain the reasons for its choice to the class.
3. After the groups have made their selections, tell them to assume that the group in the case study will not be electing the leader. Ask them to instead identify which individual in the situation would most likely emerge as the leader. The group should be prepared to explain the reasons for its answers to the class.
4. Each group should select a spokesperson. The spokesperson should announce the group's selections and explain the rationale.

TEACHING TIPS

Groups will often select a leader through a process of elimination. However, students should be encouraged to provide specific reasons to justify their selection of a particular individual. Remind students that a designated leader and an emergent leader will not always be the same person. This activity should be followed with a discussion of theories of leadership and the differences between designated and emergent leaders. Discussion questions:

- ❖ Were there certain individuals who were immediately eliminated from consideration? Why?
- ❖ Did your selected leader possess all of the traits you would have liked to see in a leader in this situation? What additional traits would make that individual a better leader?
- ❖ Did that person have any traits you would not have liked to see in this situation? Why did you select the person anyway?
- ❖ Did age, culture, or gender influence the group's decisions?
- ❖ Which leadership theory do you think best explains your group's selection?
- ❖ What differences, if any, were there between designated and emergent leaders?

CASE STUDY: DESERT ISLE

A group of seven individuals embarked on a week-long cruise aboard a chartered luxury yacht. On the third day, a severe storm caused the yacht to run aground on a deserted island. Aside from minor scratches and bruises, all crew and passengers escaped serious injury. Unfortunately, the yacht was damaged beyond repair. Furthermore, the yacht's only radio was damaged. It can receive messages but can no longer transmit messages. After several days, they hear over the radio that the effort to locate and rescue them has been abandoned. The group is presumed dead.

The island is uninhabited. There is sufficient vegetation and fresh water to sustain them indefinitely. Despite the outside world's assumption that they have died at sea, the group has resolved to find a way to return home. In the meantime, they must prepare for a life together on the island. The following people are stranded on the island:

CAPTAIN

Sixty-four years old, Captain Reynolds began offering chartered cruises to wealthy customers after retiring from the Navy. Despite the current predicament, he is considered an extremely capable captain. Unfortunately, his health has declined in the past year. He has seriously considered retirement.

FIRST MATE

Mario Gonzales is 28 years old. Since graduating from high school, he has worked as a first mate while deciding what to do with his life. Currently, he has been taking engineering courses at the local community college. Last year he was instrumental in organizing a clean-up of the beach in his neighborhood. Friends find him personable and creative.

CELEBRITY

Debra Shore is 32 years old. She is one of the world's most popular actors. She graduated from an ivy league university and finished directing her first movie. Entertainment industry people consider her easy to work with. Her fans adore her. She has been divorced four times and rumored to have a substance abuse problem. She took this trip to relax and read scripts.

PSYCHIATRIST

At 43, Dr. Margaret Finnegan has a successful private practice and two best-selling, self-help books entitled *It's Not As Bad As You Think* and *Taking Charge in Times of Crisis.* She is also the host of a national radio talk show. She was recently audited by the I.R.S. and charged with tax fraud. The case has not yet been settled. She came on this cruise as William Bates' companion.

BILLIONAIRE

At 45, William Bates is a billionaire, the result of starting a small computer software company that grew to be one of the most successful corporations in the country. His competitors consider him both brilliant and ruthless, while some former employees describe him as aloof and arrogant. He came on this cruise as Dr. Margaret Finnegan's companion.

PLASTIC SURGEON

Dr. Sang Kim is a 40 year old Korean American. After immigrating to the U.S., he attended medical school on scholarships. He graduated top in his class. Before starting a private practice in plastic surgery, he worked many hours at free clinics providing care to the poor. He is an outspoken leader within the Korean American community; however, his English is difficult to understand at times. Recently, he has been under a lot of stress and took this cruise to relax.

FACTORY WORKER

Norma Ryan is 47 years old. She began working at a factory after dropping out of high school at the age of 16. Over the years she has received praise for her hard work and has been awarded "Employee of the Year" four times. Currently, she is the leader of her local union chapter. She has also been very active in the P.T.A. All three of her children are college graduates. She won this cruise as a sweepstakes prize.

CHAPTER 8

LEADERSHIP IN GROUPS

BATTLE OF THE SEXES

GOAL

- To become aware of stereotypical beliefs regarding gender and leadership.
- To consider the influence of gender on group leadership.

PARTICIPANTS

Groups of 5 to 7 members divided by gender.

PROCEDURE

1. Divide the class into groups according to gender. If the class is small, you may divide the class into two groups according to gender.
2. Ask each group to answer the following questions:
   - What can be irritating about leaders of the opposite sex?
   - How do we think the opposite sex groups will answer the first question?
3. Groups should record their answers throughout the discussion and be prepared to present their responses to the entire class.
4. Each group should select a spokesperson to present the group's responses.
5. The male spokespersons should present their predictions of the female groups' answers to the first question.
6. The female spokespersons should then present their answers to the first question.
7. The female spokespersons should present their groups' predictions of the male groups' answers to the first question.
8. The male spokespersons should then present their groups' answers to the first question.

TEACHING TIPS

This activity can be used to introduce a discussion of the research related to gender and leadership. The length of the activity will depend on how many responses the groups are instructed to develop. Three responses to each question are sufficient for a shorter activity. Ten responses works well when more time is available. Discussion questions:

- ❖ How accurate were each group's predictions?
- ❖ Are any of these traits more characteristic of a particular gender?
- ❖ Which of these responses are gender stereotypes?
- ❖ What led you to those stereotypes? Were they the result of personal experiences, media portrayals, educational knowledge, etc.?
- ❖ Do males and females have different leadership styles or are they only perceived as different?
- ❖ How much consideration should a group give to gender when selecting a leader?

CHAPTER 8

LEADERSHIP IN GROUPS

WHAT CONSTITUTES EFFECTIVE LEADERSHIP?

GOAL

- To share and analyze common perceptions of effective leadership.

PARTICIPANTS

Groups of 5 to 7 members.

PROCEDURE

1. Distribute copies of the *Agree-Disagree Questionnaire.* Instruct each group member to complete the questionnaire individually.
2. After everyone has completed the questionnaire, members should discuss each statement and determine which answer best represents the group's collective response.
3. After the discussion, all groups should share their final rating for each statement.

TEACHING TIPS

This activity is useful as an introduction to the theories of leadership. Follow the activity with a discussion. Discussion questions:

- ❖ Which items were the most difficult for the group to reach an agreement?
- ❖ Which items were the easiest for the group to come to agreement?
- ❖ How important is leadership in groups?
- ❖ What can be the effect of a poor leader on a group?
- ❖ Did any groups find it difficult to agree upon a common rating for one or more statements? If yes, what was the basis of disagreement?
- ❖ Did any particular experiences you have had in past groups lead to your responses? If so, what were they?

AGREE-DISAGREE QUESTIONNAIRE

Circle the answer that best represents your response to each of the following statements. Do you Strongly Agree (SA), Agree (A), Neither Agree Nor Disagree (N), Disagree (D), or Strongly Disagree (SD) with each statement about leadership?

SA A N D SD 1. When a group is unable to solve a problem or make a decision about an important issue, an effective leader should take over and make the decision for the group.

SA A N D SD 2. An effective group leader should keep the discussion organized and progressing toward the group's goal rather than actively participate in the discussion.

SA A N D SD 3. An effective group leader should learn as much as possible about the personal lives and interests of group members in order to understand and respond to their needs.

SA A N D SD 4. When a group member causes serious problems or threatens the group's success, an effective leader will confront the member with the problem.

SA A N D SD 5. When a group needs direction, an effective leader should call attention to the tasks that need to be done by assigning responsibilities to different group members.

SA A N D SD 6. An effective leader should try to establish a friendly atmosphere among the members of the group.

SA A N D SD 7. An effective leader is persistent, intelligent, self-confident, persuasive, willing to accept the consequences of actions, and able to withstand stress and tolerate frustration.

SA A N D SD 8. When the members of a group are cooperative, motivated, and very able, an effective leader should back off and follow the group's lead.

CHAPTER 8

LEADERSHIP IN GROUPS

EXTRAORDINARY LEADERS

GOALS

- To identify leadership models for class discussion.
- To discern some of the differences between "good" and "bad" leaders.
- To discuss the implications of Trait Theory.

PARTICIPANTS

Groups of 5 to 7 members.

PROCEDURE

1. Ask students to spend a few minutes thinking about extraordinary leaders from the beginning of time to today.
2. Tell students to write their top five extraordinary leaders on a piece of paper. They may not choose someone they know personally.
3. Divide students into work groups to compare their lists. Students should then generate the characteristics they believe to have been typical of extraordinary leaders.
4. After completing the group discussion, a spokesperson should report to the class.

TEACHING TIPS

This is a good introductory exercise for the unit on group leadership. Most students can identify five extraordinary leaders. Encourage them to think about leaders from the beginning of time to today. Although individual lists will vary, some leaders will appear on several lists. Very often, student lists will include leaders such as Adolph Hitler. Examples of "bad" leaders can prompt a discussion about the nature of leadership and the need to be wary of charismatic leaders. The discussion of leader characteristics can illustrate why it is difficult to come up with a universal list of leadership qualities and skills. This discussion can also lead to a discussion of other leadership theories that consider the nature of the leadership task and the circumstances under which a leader must lead. Discussion questions:

- ❖ How many extraordinary leaders appeared on more than one list?
- ❖ Were there any surprising selections?
- ❖ Who are the group's top five extraordinary leaders?
- ❖ What are some of the common characteristics of these extraordinary leaders?
- ❖ Were all of these leaders "good" people? If not, what conclusion can you draw from that?

CHAPTER 8

LEADERSHIP IN GROUPS

THEY DROVE ME CRAZY

GOAL

- To get students to identify the negative characteristics of leaders that have an adverse impact on group functioning.

PARTICIPANTS

Groups of 5 to 6 people.

PROCEDURE

1. Divide the class into groups of 5 to 6 people and have them discuss the characteristics of the worst leaders they have personally interacted with. Those leaders may be employers, teachers, etc. You may provide some starting examples such as egomaniac, dictator, doormat, unprepared, etc.
2. Have each group prepare a list of five of the most common negative characteristics.
3. Have a spokesperson from each group present the list to the class. You may want to write the responses on the blackboard.

TEACHING TIPS

Rather than focusing on the positive characteristics of leaders, this exercise allows a discussion of those characteristics that can impede effective leadership. A variation of this exercise could be done to focus on the negative characteristics of those in subordinate positions. Discussion questions:

- What seem to be the most common problematic characteristics of leaders?
- Would these characteristics be problems in all group situations?
- How did these characteristics impact the group process?
- Could the group have done anything to minimize the problems?

CHAPTER 9

DECISION MAKING AND PROBLEM SOLVING IN GROUPS

GAME BUILDING

GOAL

- To demonstrate the value of creative problem solving.

PARTICIPANTS

Groups of 5 to 7 members.

PROCEDURE

This exercise is provided in the Groupwork section of the chapter.

1. Each group receives the following items:
   - One overhead transparency sheet
   - A marker
   - A bag filled with game components such as 10 large, soft plastic jacks of varying colors, 5 marbles, one large superball, or marble, etc.
2. Groups have 30 minutes to create a game using all the items and to write the rules of the game on a single transparency.
3. A spokesperson or spokesperson(s) from each group presents the game and its rules to the rest of the class. The rules must fit on one transparency.

TEACHING TIPS

While this exercise primarily focuses on the use of creativity, it also allows for participation by students whose orientation tends to be more linear. Discussion questions:

- ❖ What types of creative thinking were evident in the group?
- ❖ Were some members better skilled at creative thinking, at organizing the group task, at expressing the rules, or at making the presentation?
- ❖ Did the group benefit from having individuals with different orientations toward solving the problem?
- ❖ In what group situations or jobs would these skills be needed or useful?

CHAPTER 9

DECISION MAKING AND PROBLEM SOLVING IN GROUPS

LOST ON THE MOON

GOAL

- To demonstrate the advantages and disadvantages of group problem solving.

PARTICIPANTS

Groups of 5 to 7 members.

PROCEDURE

1. Each group member should complete the individual worksheet without help from or discussion with other group members. The worksheet also appears in the textbook.
2. After everyone has completed the individual worksheet, group members should share their answers and agree upon a group ranking of items that best satisfies all group members.
3. Groups should be encouraged to use the guidelines for seeking consensus when discussing and making their decisions.
4. After all groups have reached consensus, the correct answers and their rationale should be distributed or announced to score the worksheets.
5. To calculate final scores, instruct students to complete the following steps:
   - To calculate individual scores, determine the error points for each item by calculating the difference between the correct answer and your individual answer. For example, NASA ranks food concentrate #4. If you were to rank it #6, your error points for that item would equal 2.
   - After identifying the error points for each item, add them together to determine your total individual score.
   - Calculate the group's score by determining the error points between NASA's answers and the group's rankings. Add the points together to determine the group's final score.
6. Ask group members to compare their individual scores with each other and the final group score.
7. Announce the following interpretation of the scores: (NASA's scores are for individuals.)

0 - 25	Excellent
26- 32	Good
33 - 45	Average
46 - 55	Fair
56 - 70	Poor
71 - 112	Very Poor

TEACHING TIPS

Occasionally, an individual group member will score better than the group as a whole. If that occurs, have the student's assess what happened in the group. Discussion questions:

- ❖ Who was more likely to survive, individuals working alone or groups?
- ❖ Why did the groups rank the items more accurately?
- ❖ Were there specific instances in which a member's specialized knowledge, creativity, or common sense caused the group to see an item differently?
- ❖ In what types of situations are groups better than individuals at problem solving?

LOST ON THE MOON WORKSHEET

INSTRUCTIONS: You are a member of a space crew originally scheduled to rendezvous with a mother ship on the lighted surface of the moon. Due to mechanical difficulties, however, your ship crash-landed on a lighted spot some 200 miles from the rendezvous point. During landing, much of the equipment aboard was damaged and, since survival depends on reaching the mother ship, the most critical items available must be chosen for the 200-mile trip. Below are listed the 15 items left intact and undamaged after landing. Your task is to rank order them in terms of their importance to your crew in allowing them to reach the rendezvous point. Place the number 1 by the most important item, the number 2 by the second most important, and so on, through number 15, the least important.

ITEM	Your Rankings	Group Rankings	NASA Rankings	Your Error Points	Group Error Points
Box of matches					
Food concentrates					
Fifty feet of nylon rope					
Parachute silk					
Solar-powered portable heating unit					
Two .45-caliber pistols					
One case of dehydrated milk					
Two 100-pound tanks of oxygen					
Stellar map (of the moon's constellations)					
Self-inflating life raft					
Magnetic compass					
Five gallons of water					
Signal flares					
First-aid kit containing injection needles					
Solar-powered FM receiver-transmitter					

Your Score= _____ Group Score= _____

LOST ON THE MOON

ANSWERS AND RATIONALE

ITEM	ANSWER	RATIONALE
Box of matches	15	No oxygen on the moon
Food concentrates	4	Efficient means of supplying energy
Fifty feet of nylon rope	6	Useful for scaling cliffs or tying injured together
Parachute silk	8	Protection from sun
Solar-powered portable heating unit	13	Not necessary on the lighted side
Two .45-caliber pistols	11	Means of self-propulsion
One case of dehydrated milk	12	Bulkier than the food concentrate
Two 100-pound tanks of oxygen	1	Most critical survival need
Stellar map (of the moon's constellations)	3	Primary means of navigation
Self-inflating life raft	9	CO_2 bottle is a means of propulsion
Magnetic compass	14	Worthless for navigation; magnetic field on moon is not polarized.
Five gallons of water	2	Replacement for fluid loss
Signal flares	10	Distress signal when mother ship is sighted
First-aid kit containing injection needles	7	Needles for vitamins and medicine will fit apertures in space suits
Solar-powered FM receiver-transmitter	5	For communication with mother ship; FM requires short-range transmission

CHAPTER 9

DECISION MAKING AND PROBLEM SOLVING IN GROUPS

OZONE COLLAPSE SCENARIO

GOALS

- To practice The Standard Agenda approach to problem solving and decision making.
- To practice developing criteria for making group decisions.

PARTICIPANTS

Groups of 5 to 7 members.

PROCEDURE

1. Distribute copies of the *Ozone Collapse Scenario* and the accompanying *Potential Survivors* handout.
2. Instruct students to seek consensus as they decide who will be chosen as survivors in the scenario. Groups should follow The Standard Agenda approach to problem solving presented in the textbook.
3. Remind the groups of the importance of developing clear criteria for their selections.
4. After all groups have finalized their decisions, each group should select a spokesperson.
5. Each spokesperson should briefly present to the entire class the criteria developed and the selections made by his or her group.

TEACHING TIPS

This is a lengthy activity and may take an entire class session. Consider distributing the scenario with the list of potential survivors in advance. Tell students to consider the problem posed in the scenario before the next class session. The activity can be shortened by providing students with a shorter list of potential survivors. Instead of assigning The Standard Agenda approach, Hirokawa's functional approach could be used. Discussion questions:

- ❖ Did the selected survivors meet the criteria developed by the group?
- ❖ Did the criteria change during the discussion?
- ❖ Did you feel pressure from the group to agree to certain decisions?
- ❖ What was the most difficult decision?

This is a condensed version of an activity created by Dr. Todd Holm. A more fully developed version of the activity is available. For information or to request a copy, contact Dr. Todd Holm at:

Truman State University
McClain Hall 310
Kirksville, MO 63501
todd@truman.edu

OZONE COLLAPSE SCENARIO

The ozone protecting the Earth has been slowly weakened by environmental abuse over the last fifty years. An explosion at an aerosol spray can manufacturing plant and warehouse has dealt the last devastating blow to the planet's already depleted ozone layer. Total collapse is imminent within one hour. The devastation will be a holocaust. Every living plant, animal, and insect (with the possible exception of cockroaches) will die.

The only possible protection from this catastrophe is the Biosphere II Project. Biosphere II is an artificial Earth simulation project in the middle of the desert. It is an enclosed one square mile area. The sphere is large enough that rain showers inside the structure are frequent and the vegetation produces all of the oxygen needed for the animals and ten people to survive. With time and increased vegetation, more people would be able to survive. However, for the time being, only ten people may remain inside the structure.

A variety of insects and animals are present inside the structure including: cows, two horses, pigs, sheep, chickens, a few birds, a bee hive, and a variety of flying and crawling insects.

Your group has been chosen to select the survivors because you are among the world's most intelligent people. Sorry, you cannot save yourselves. You live too far from Biosphere to get there before the ozone layer collapses. Your mission is to determine which ten people will survive to rebuild the planet.

POTENTIAL SURVIVORS

NAME	Sex	Age	Occupation	Personal Traits
Father Thyme	M	35	Catholic Priest	Familiar with many religions; good religious leader, teacher, and carpenter; well liked; would have to break his vow of celibacy.
Daisy Smith	F	25	Botanist	Friendly and in good health, but her father had polio; well respected in field of botany.
General Rock	M	45	Military Leader	Expert in guerrilla warfare; strong leader; military's youngest general ever; a West Point graduate.
Melody Score	F	22	Singer/Artist	Sculptor, singer, songwriter, and poet; composed her first published song at the age of 14; currently working on her first full-length novel.
Sigmund Quark	M	30	Psychiatrist	Specializes in phobias and paranoia; confined to a wheel chair for 11 years because of a car crash; still functions sexually.
Dr. No Name	M	33	Doctor (?)	Does not speak English and other group members don't speak his language; may be a doctor, but could be a nurse; has some medical training.
Grease McKay	M	19	Mechanic	Can fix anything; a bit of a hothead; has been accused of sexual harassment.
Manny Labor	M	24	Construction Worker	Outspoken; excellent carpentry and construction skills; appears to be in good health but smokes cigars; swears a lot and could shower more often.
Edger Hear	M	22	Computer Whiz	Exceptional computer skills; hacked into the Treasury Department's computer system for fun; skinny, weak, and anemic; spends his time reading.
Tea Chure	F	23	Elementary School Teacher	Good teacher; well liked; is a manic depressive and needs professional counseling.
Mary Burger	F	22	Fast Food Attendant	In her last semester of college studying Animal Science; plans to enter veterinary school; openly bisexual.
Jeanie Tracker	F	45	Geneticist	Authority on genetics, gene splicing, cloning and heredity; familiar with selective breeding techniques for preventing birth defects.
Sgt. Trusty	M	27	Police Officer	Walks a beat in the inner city; has been accused of police brutality four times, but has never been convicted; received the Medal of Valor.
Libby Rarman	F	26	Librarian	Timid and shy; graduated at the top of her class with a masters degree in Library Science; exceptional organizational skills and record keeping abilities.
Enos Howell	M	25	Corporate Manager	Abrasive personality; very good at getting the job done; keeps an eye on the bottom line; great manager.
Prof. Dulman	F	35	Professor	Teaches mathematics at an ivy league university. very knowledgeable, but lectures are extremely boring.
Betty Jo Hicks	F	20	Farmer	Pleasant person; poor student in high school; lived on a farm all of her life and knows a lot about raising crops and animals.
Charles Slick	M	35	Politician	Former ambassador, congressman, and committee chair; hopes to run for president in a few years; well liked by voters; always has landslide victories.
Ms. Wright	F	27	Women's Rights Activist	Assertive; negative attitude toward men; divorced three times; good physical health.

CHAPTER 9

DECISION MAKING AND PROBLEM SOLVING IN GROUPS

PLANNING WITH PERT

GOAL

- To practice using the PERT method for planning group projects.

PARTICIPANTS

Groups of 4 to 6 members.

PROCEDURE

1. Inform students that they will be planning a hypothetical event following the PERT guidelines presented in the textbook.
2. Review the PERT guidelines.
3. Groups should work together to plan one of the following events:
   - a neighborhood clean-up
   - a group outing to a sports event (e.g. a baseball game)
   - selection of the graduation speaker
   - a class food drive for Thanksgiving
4. Each group should elect a spokesperson. After the groups have completed the PERT process, each spokesperson should present a summary of his or her group's plan.

TEACHING TIPS

Another option is to assign all of the groups the same event to plan. The results of each group can then be compared at the end of the activity. This activity works best after students are familiar with the PERT process. Discussion questions:

- ❖ What was the most difficult step of the process? Why?
- ❖ If you had been working individually rather than in groups, do you think some details might have been forgotten?
- ❖ In what type of situations would PERT be useful?
- ❖ Why does the PERT process help a group implement its plans?

CHAPTER 9

DECISION MAKING AND PROBLEM SOLVING IN GROUPS

SELLING THE BROOKLYN BRIDGE

GOAL

- To encourage creative thinking in group problem solving.

PARTICIPANTS

Groups of 5 to 7 members.

PROCEDURE

1. Present the following situation to the groups:

   The Brooklyn Bridge is no longer structurally sound. Thus, the bridge is going to be dismantled and replaced with a new bridge. The city would like to recover a portion of the cost of this project by selling all or part of the structure. Your group is responsible for identifying another use for the bridge that will allow the city to sell it. The bridge can be sold as is or in smaller sections. The only limitation is that it cannot be sold for use as a bridge.

2. Instruct groups to discuss the situation and generate a variety of possible ideas for new uses for the bridge. Groups should then discuss their ideas and choose one.
3. Once groups have developed an idea for a new use for the bridge, they should then discuss strategies for selling it.
4. Each group should select a spokesperson to "sell" the bridge to the class.

TEACHING TIPS

You could choose other national or local landmarks in place of the Brooklyn Bridge for this activity. Another option is to bring to class a variety of objects. Each group receives a different object to sell as a product to be used for a purpose for which it was not originally intended. Encourage outrageous ideas as the groups discuss their options.
Discussion questions:

- How difficult was it to come up with creative ideas?
- Could any of the ideas presented in class actually be used?
- Did the group seem to have fun with the problem?
- How important is creativity to problem solving?
- What types of behavior tend to discourage creative thinking in a group?
- What types of behavior tend to encourage creative thinking in a group?

CHAPTER 9

DECISION MAKING AND PROBLEM SOLVING IN GROUPS

SO THAT'S WHAT IT MEANS

GOAL

- To give students an opportunity to think logically and creatively
- To allow students to see the benefits of group input

PARTICIPANTS

Groups of 4 to 5 members.

PROCEDURE

1. Distribute the *So That's What it Means* handout to the class and divide the class into groups of 4 to 5 members.
2. Give students 5 to 10 minutes to complete the exercise.
3. Ask the class for the answers. Provide any answers to those items the groups did not figure out.

TEACHING TIPS

This is a simple exercise that allows for a fair amount of group interaction. Some students will see answers quickly that others really puzzle over. It provides opportunities to discuss why people see things differently when attempting to solve a problem. Discussion questions:

- ❖ Were some problems easier to solve than others were? Why?
- ❖ Did some individuals see solutions more quickly than others?
- ❖ Did anything in your personal background lead you to see solutions that others did not?

SO THAT'S WHAT IT MEANS

The following list contains a series of well-known phrases and concepts. You are to identify what each means. Do not think of it as a test of your intelligence or your ability with language.

Example: 26=L of the A 26 Letters of the Alphabet

1. 7=W of the AW ______
2. 1,001=AN ______
3. 12=S of the Z ______
4. 54=C in a D (With the J's) ______
5. 9=P in the SS ______
6. 88=PK ______
7. 13=S on the AF ______
8. 32 =D at which WF ______
9. 18=H on a GC ______
10. 1=RA in EB ______
11. 200=D for PG in M ______
12. 3=BM (SHTR) ______
13. 9=J of the SC ______
14. 3=SYO at the the OBG ______
15. 5=D in a ZC ______
16. 57=HV ______
17. 11=P on a FT ______
18. 1000=W a P is W ______
19. 29=D in F in a LY ______
20. 64=S on a C ______

ANSWER SHEET FOR "SO THAT'S WHAT IT MEANS"

1. 7 Wonders of the Ancient World
2. 1001 Arabian Nights
3. 12 Signs of the Zodiac
4. 54 Cards in a Deck (with the Jokers)
5. 7 Planets in the Solar System
6. 88 Piano Keys
7. 13 Stripes on the American Flag
8. 32 Degrees at which Water Freezes
9. 18 Holes on a Golf Course
10. 1 Rotten Apple in Every Barrel
11. 200 Dollars for Passing Go in Monopoly
12. 3 Blind Mice (See How They Run)
13. 9 Justices of the Supreme Court
14. 3 Strikes and You're Out at the Old Ball Game
15. 5 Digits in a Zip Code
16. 57 Heinz Varieties
17. 11 Players on a Football Team
18. 1000 Words a Picture is Worth
19. 29 Days in February in a Leap Year
20. 64 Squares on a Checkerboard

CHAPTER 9

DECISION MAKING AND PROBLEM SOLVING IN GROUPS

ONE STEP AT A TIME

GOAL

- To allow students to use both logic and creativity in problem solving.

PARTICIPANTS

Groups of 5 to 6 members.

PROCEDURE

1. Ask the class to randomly call out a series of ten nouns. Write them on the far left side of the blackboard. Then have them randomly call out a series of ten different nouns and write them on the far right side of the blackboard.
2. Divide the class into groups of 5 to 6 and distribute the *One Step at a Time* handout. Have the students fill in the far left and right columns so that it matches the blackboard.
3. Inform them that their task is to link the two items on each line. The middle three words should be filled in so that each word is somehow logically connected to the word to its left. The last word in the far right column need not have any relationship to the word in column 1, only to the word immediately preceding it.

TEACHING TIPS

This exercise can illustrate how both logical and creative thought may be involved in problem solving. Some students may be better at one than the other, but a group generally benefits from the presence of both types. Discussion questions:

- ❖ Were certain linkages easier than others? Why?
- ❖ Would you consider your own attempts at solving the problem more linear or more creative?
- ❖ Did other group members see connections that were not immediately obvious to you?
- ❖ What implications for group processing can you draw from this?

ONE STEP AT A TIME

The nouns called out in class should be placed in the far left and far right columns. Your task is to fill in the three blank lines with a new word that is logically related or associated with the one immediately preceding it. Remember that the final word need not be related to the word in column 1, only to the word in column 4.
Example:

Teacher				**Safari**
Teacher	Vacation	Travel	Africa	**Safari**

Random Nouns				**Random Nouns**

CHAPTER 10

ARGUMENTATION IN GROUPS

DIVIDE AND DEBATE

GOAL

- To practice argumentation skills in a group setting.

PARTICIPANTS

Groups of 5 to 7 members.

PROCEDURE

This exercise is provided in the Groupwork section of the chapter.

1. Approximately half the members of each group (the pro side) should be assigned to present arguments in support of the following claim: "It is better to work in groups than it is to work individually." The other half of the group (the con side) should oppose the claim.
2. Allow group members to consult the textbook for evidence in support of their arguments.
3. Groups are to adhere to the following format for discussion:

Pro Side	4 minutes
Con Side	4 minutes
Pro Side	2 minutes
Con Side	4 minutes
Pro Side	2 minutes

4. Remind students to follow the guidelines discussed in Chapter 10 for presenting and refuting arguments.
5. All members of the group should be encouraged to participate.

TEACHING TIPS

This activity works well after students are familiar with the steps for presenting and refuting arguments explained in the textbook. Discussion questions:

- ❖ How difficult was it for members to make their points within the time limitations?
- ❖ Was it difficult to refrain from interrupting members presenting opposing ideas?
- ❖ How effectively did group members use evidence from the textbook to support their claims?
- ❖ How effectively did group members respond to opposition arguments?
- ❖ Who won the debate? Why?

CHAPTER 10

ARGUMENTATION IN GROUPS

GROUP DEBATE

GOALS

- To provide students with an opportunity to develop an argument as a group.
- To practice presenting arguments briefly and concisely.
- To practice the skills of refutation.

PARTICIPANTS

The entire class divided into two large groups.

PROCEDURE

1. Students should divide into two large groups. The groups should be located as far away from each other as possible. Each group should sit in a circle.
2. Inform the groups that they will be debating the following topic: "Possession of hand guns and assault rifles by private citizens should be banned."
3. Assign one group to argue in favor of the claim and the other group to oppose it.
4. Allow each group five minutes to discuss the arguments it wants to present.
5. Inform the class that all group members will have an opportunity to present an argument. The members should determine the sequence in which they will speak.
6. The group arguing in support of the claim presents the first argument. The opposing group then responds. The groups continue taking turns in this manner throughout the activity.
7. The first speaker of each group should be allowed two minutes to overview his or her group's arguments.
8. Each subsequent speaker will be given 30 seconds to present an argument and/or respond to an argument posed by the other group.

TEACHING TIPS

Instruct students not to interrupt each other during the other group's speaking time. Strictly enforcing the 30-second speaking time limit encourages students to make a point more concisely. As the activity progresses, they should improve their ability to present a clear argument. The activity can be stopped after all members have spoken or can continue through several speaking turns as class time permits. Follow the activity with a discussion of the nature of argumentation in groups. Discussion questions:

- How difficult was it to present your arguments within the time limit?
- When a member spends a lot of time presenting an argument, how do you think other group members respond?
- Did class members effectively listen to the arguments of the other members?
- Did anyone respond to the arguments of others? What impact did that have?
- How difficult was it to argue without having an opportunity to research?
- Which side won the debate? Why?

CHAPTER 10

ARGUMENTATION IN GROUPS

CLASS CODE OF ETHICS

GOALS

- To promote a discussion of ethics.
- To develop a "Code of Ethics" that students will adhere to when working in groups.

PARTICIPANTS

Groups of 4 to 6 members.

PROCEDURE

1. Review the following four ethical responsibilities identified in the textbook:
   - The Research Responsibility
   - The Common Good Responsibility
   - The Reasoning Responsibility
   - The Social Code Responsibility
2. Instruct each group to develop at least two rules for each responsibility that class members should follow when working in groups.
3. After the groups have developed their rules, members should select a leader to represent them.
4. The leader should then meet with the leaders of the other groups. Instruct them to develop one "Code of Ethics" document for the entire class based upon the work done by their groups. They may modify, combine, eliminate, or add items to create their document.
5. The leaders should return to their group and present the document. Group members may approve, disapprove, or suggest changes to the document.
6. Instruct the leaders to meet with each other a second time to finalize the "Code of Ethics."
7. The final product should be read aloud to the class. Explain to the class that these are the rules that everyone will be expected to follow when in class or working in groups.

TEACHING TIPS

This activity encourages students to think about the differences between acceptable and unacceptable behaviors. Allowing the students to develop the rules increases the likelihood that they will adhere to them. Consider typing the class's "Code of Ethics" and distributing copies of it at the next class session. Discussion questions:

- ❖ Which rules do you think are the most important?
- ❖ Which rules do groups tend to violate the most?
- ❖ How can a "Code of Ethics" improve a group?
- ❖ What should a group do to a member who is found in violation of one of the rules?

CHAPTER 10

ARGUMENTATION IN GROUPS

RED ROVER, RED ROVER

GOALS

- To provide students an opportunity to practice arguing.

PARTICIPANTS

Entire class.

PROCEDURE

1. Write a series of questions on which students are likely to disagree. You may choose either current events questions (e.g., "The United States should invade Iraq.") or questions related to course materials (e.g., "Most people are good at reading nonverbal signals.") Avoid using absolute words such as "all," "never," etc. Be prepared to adjust the topic wording midway through the exercise.
2. Place the following signs on the four walls of the classroom: "Strongly Agree," "Agree," "Strongly Disagree," and "Disagree." The "Strong" responses should be opposite one another.
3. Have each student move to the side of the room that best represents the student's initial position.
4. Have students make arguments to the other groups. Students who are persuaded by an argument should move to that side of the room.

TEACHING TIPS

Give sufficient time for each question but do not allow it to become belabored; move to a new question when the process seems to be slowing. Act as a facilitator only but attempt to involve all students. Make sure students address one another, not the instructor. Do not allow students to stand in the middle of the room. Discussion questions:

- ❖ What caused some of you to move? What kept others of you from moving?
- ❖ How did you feel when someone moved after your argument? How did you feel when no one moved?
- ❖ Why were people who moved more likely to move slightly rather than make dramatic moves?
- ❖ How did the lack of research on the topic impact the ability to make a persuasive argument?

Note: This exercise can be used at any point in the semester if you are asking questions related to the specific topic area.

CHAPTER 11

MOTIVATING GROUPS

YOUR GUIDING MOTIVE

GOALS

- To help group members identify the major factors that motivate their work.
- To demonstrate the diversity of motivating factors within a single group.
- To focus group attention on *intrinsic* rewards as sources of motivation.

PARTICIPANTS

Entire class and groups of 5 to 7 members

PROCEDURE

1. Give each class member seven 3 x 5 index cards. Then ask them to write each of the following six words on six different cards: Achievement, Recognition, Work Itself, Responsibility, Advancement, and Growth.
2. Distribute the *Guiding Motives Information Sheet* as a way of explaining the basic characteristics of each motive.
3. If students believe they are motivated by something other than the six guiding motives, ask them to write that motive on the 7th index card with a few words *explaining* the motive's unique qualities.
4. Tell students to think about the 6 or 7 motives and discard the three that are least important to them. Then ask them to think about the *remaining* motives and discard another one or two so that they have only two motive cards remaining.
5. Form groups of 5 to 7 members. Ask students to choose the least important of the final two cards and to take turns answering the following questions:
   - Why is this motive important to you?
   - How does this motive affect your participation in groups?
   - How can groups use this motive to motivate your behavior?
6. Conduct a second round in which members discuss their final and most important personal motive. Ask students to answer the three questions listed above.
7. Ask all the groups to share their top motives with the class. Discuss their similarities and differences.

TEACHING TIPS

Discussion questions:

- ❖ Which, if any, motives were most frequently chosen by group members?
- ❖ How can the group enlist the most frequently chosen motives to enhance group productivity and member satisfaction?
- ❖ If one or two members have unique motives, how can the group enlist these motives to enhance group work?

The six motives listed on the Guiding Motives Information sheet are based on Frederick Herzberg's research of employee motivation.[1] In looking for factors that affect employee attitudes about work, he came up with two sets of motives. One set of factors led to extreme dissatisfaction (examples: company policies & administration; supervision, working conditions, pay and benefits, relationships with peers and subordinates). None of these factors motivate. Although satisfying them may remove unhappiness, they are only prerequisites for motivation. A second set of factors led to extreme job satisfaction. These factors motivate. They are closely related to Maslow's esteem and self-actualization needs. The six top factors appear on the *Guiding Motives Information Sheet*.

Please note that Herzberg's categories are used in this exercise as a convenient way of initiating a class discussion about member motivation. Since being published, Herzberg's model has lost some of its credibility when subsequent empirical studies failed to support all of its claims. In *Working in Groups,* we use Kenneth Thomas's four intrinsic motivators (a sense of meaningfulness, a sense of choice, a sense of competence, and a sense of progress) as a model of motivation. Although the Herzberg and Thomas models have many elements in common, the Herzberg model works more effectively in this classroom exercise.

If, after conducting this exercise several times, the guiding motives do not work for your class, develop your own list. Pay careful attention to the additional motives selected by students. There are no right or wrong answers in this exercise so feel free to modify it to suit your needs.

[1] See Herzberg, F., Mausner, B. & Snydermann, B. (1959). *The motivation to work.* New York: Wiley; Herzberg, F. (1968). " One more time, How do you motivate employees?" *Harvard Business Review.* The Guiding Motives Information Sheet is modeled on an exercise from Frazer-Robinson, J. (1999). *Mastering motivation.* Pembury, England: David Grand Publishing, pp. 32-33.

THE GUIDING MOTIVES INFORMATION SHEET

ACHIEVEMENT

- ❑ Personal contributions to the group's goal
- ❑ Knowledge
- ❑ Abilities and skills
- ❑ High standards for work
- ❑ Self-created, personal goals

RECOGNITION

- ❑ Receive regular, constructive feedback
- ❑ Praise for accomplishments
- ❑ Awards, honors, celebrations
- ❑ Status and job titles
- ❑ Salary increases and bonuses

THE WORK ITSELF

- ❑ Challenging and interesting work
- ❑ Involvement in group decisions
- ❑ Freedom to work in your own way
- ❑ Measurable standards of performance
- ❑ Clear, relevant, and worthy goals

RESPONSIBILITY

- ❑ Authority to act
- ❑ Involvement in planning
- ❑ Access to information and experts
- ❑ Less supervision
- ❑ Trust of your ability and commitment

ADVANCEMENT

- ❑ Leadership assignments
- ❑ Job prestige, status, perks
- ❑ Promotion
- ❑ Career success
- ❑ Management and supervision responsibilities

PERSONAL GROWTH

- ❑ Self-knowledge
- ❑ Continuous learning and improvement
- ❑ Long-term personal goals
- ❑ Personal confidence
- ❑ Creativity and invention

CHAPTER 11

MOTIVATING GROUP

IT WAS THE BEST OF TEAMS

GOALS

- To understand the ways in which work can motivate and reward.
- To distinguish the differences between intrinsic and extrinsic motivators.

PARTICIPANTS

Groups of 5 to7 members

PROCEDURE

1. Before breaking into groups, ask students to think of the best group experience they ever had. Examples might be a group project on the job, an athletic team, a volunteer group, a campus club, or a service organization.
2. Students should list three reasons why they chose this group experience as so positive, enjoyable, and memorable. What did they like best about the group and its task? What made them feel valued? What did they expect from the experience? How were their expectations met? Then ask them to think about the worst group experience they ever had and answer this question: How was it different from the best group experience.
3. Break the class into groups of 5-7 members. Ask members to share, in turn, a reason why the good group experience was so positive. Someone in the group should record the reasons. Keep going around the group until everyone has shared all of their reasons and perhaps thought of some more as they hear other group members speak.
4. Ask each group to report their findings to the entire class.

TEACHING TIPS

Everyone has held a job or worked with a group they liked and one they disliked. By focusing on the characteristics of the best group experiences, class members should discover that these groups met many of their belonging, esteem, and self-actualization needs. Depending on the list generated by the class, the instructor can discuss them in light of several concepts discussed in the chapter such as: (1) Maslow, Schutz, or Myers-Briggs® categories, (2) Thomas's sense of meaningfulness, choice, competence, and progress, (3) intrinsic vs. extrinsic motivators, and (4) types of rewards. Discussion questions:

- ❖ What were some of the most commonly shared reasons?
- ❖ What kinds of motivators are implied by these reasons?
- ❖ Were the motivators absent from the group experiences they disliked?

CHAPTER 11

MOTIVATING GROUP

TIME OUT TO CELEBRATE!

GOALS

- To appreciate the need for group recognition and celebration as a motivational tool.
- To overcome barriers to celebrating group accomplishments.

PARTICIPANTS

The entire class and groups of 3 to 5 members

PROCEDURE

1. Begin the class by discussing the value of celebrating good group work. Ask the class to generate some of the ways groups can celebrate their accomplishments. Examples: Parties at work, free meals for the group, time off, off-duty get-togethers, fun "prizes," awards ceremonies.
2. Ask the class to generate some of the reasons why groups don't celebrate their success. They may provide reasons such as "It's childish," "Celebrating takes away time from work," and "It's not right to brag."
3. Divide the class into small groups of 3 to 5 members and assign at least one of the excuses for not celebrating to each group. Ask each group to come up with answers to the objection(s). A group spokesperson should be prepared to provide the group's justifications.
4. At the end of the discussion, take a few minutes to celebrate. Hand out treats, dismiss the class early, or promise a party later in the semester (and keep your promise).

TEACHING TIPS

If the class is having difficulty generating answers to celebration objections, use the following responses to illustrate the counterarguments against celebrating. (1) It's Childish: The childlike part of us is the part that gets enthusiastic and excited about things. Use this energy, excitement, and joy to motivate your group. (2) Celebrating Takes Time Away from Work: If you don't stop to smell the roses and enjoy your success, your group may burn out. Pace yourself and your group. As they say, all work and no play makes Jack (and Jill) a dull boy (and girl). Think of celebration as investments and renewals, and an insurance against burnout. (3) It's Not Right to Brag: Some groups are concerned about appearing prideful or provoking jealously and resentment from others. Remember that bragging is about how great the group is, not about showing how one person is better than another. Discussion questions:

❖ What are the links between celebration and motivation?
❖ How do celebrations meet individual and group needs?

CHAPTER 11

MOTIVATING GROUPS

CANDYGRAM

GOAL

- To allow students to see the impact of positive feedback on the group climate.

PARTICIPANTS

Entire class

PROCEDURE

1. The class should be given 5 to 10 minutes to write as many positive compliments to as many people in the class as they can. The compliments may be surface comments or deeper ones, depending on the comfort level of the sender. The notes should be anonymous.
2. Students should then deliver the notes to the recipients. The notes should be folded and no verbal exchange should take place when they are being handed over but the sender must make eye contact with the recipient. No notes should be opened until the process is complete.
3. You may wish to make observations about the nonverbal signals as the class is circulating around the room.
4. After all notes have been distributed, students may sit down to "unwrap" their presents.

TEACHING TIPS

You may wish to make comparative observations to the class about the general climate in the class at the beginning of the exercise, midway through it, and after the messages have been read. Discussion questions:

- ❖ Why is it hard for us to give compliments? Why do we not do it more often?
- ❖ Is it hard to receive compliments? How did you feel when reading what people wrote about you?
- ❖ Did the fact that they were anonymous have any impact? Why?
- ❖ Did you receive any notes from anyone you didn't give one to? How did that make you feel?
- ❖ Did you make any observations about the nonverbal behaviors as the notes were being handed out?

CHAPTER 12

INFORMED GROUPS

RESEARCH SCAVENGER HUNT

GOAL

- To practice group research techniques.

PARTICIPANTS

Groups of 5 to 7 members

PROCEDURE

This exercise is provided in the Groupwork section of the chapter.

1. Distribute a copy of the *Scavenger Hunt Questions* to all students. The questions also appear in the textbook. However, it may be easier for students to work with a separate copy of the questions when searching for answers.
2. Allow groups 10 minutes to develop an action plan for answering all questions on the list.
3. Inform the groups that they will have 30 minutes to collect as many answers as they can and return to the classroom by the deadline. (The instructor may change the time limit depending on available class time and size of campus).
4. Upon returning to the classroom, allow groups 5 minutes to compile their answers onto a single group answer sheet.

TEACHING TIPS

To motivate students to work quickly, consider offering extra credit to the group that accurately answers the most items in the fastest time. Discussion questions:

- ❖ Which questions were the most difficult to answer? Why?
- ❖ Which questions were easy to answer? Why?
- ❖ Were the answers to all of the questions found in the library?
- ❖ Was it more efficient to work as a group to locate the answers? Would you have preferred to work individually? Why or why not?
- ❖ If you had it to do over again, what might the group do differently?

SCAVENGER HUNT QUESTIONS

1. Locate an article in a magazine or newspaper about conducting effective business meetings.

   Article Title:

   Title and Date of Magazine or Newspaper:

2. What is the population of Texas?

   Population:

   Source:

3. Locate the title of a book about AIDS in your library's on-line or card catalog.

   Title of Book:

   Call Number:

4. Who is the current U. S. Secretary of Education?

   Name:

   Source:

5. How long has your college's current president served in that office?

   Answer:

   Source:

6. In what year did the U. S. Supreme Court hand down its decision in *Miranda v. Arizona?*

   Year:

   Source:

7. On what date was the charter of the United Nations approved?

   Date:

   Source:

8. What Shakespearean character said, "All the world's a stage?" What was the play?

   Character:

   Play:

CHAPTER 12

INFORMED GROUPS

A MEETING OF MINDS

GOAL

- To demonstrate the value of collaboration and information when working in groups.

PARTICIPANTS

Groups of 5 to 7 members

PROCEDURE

1. Before class develop a list of at least ten general knowledge or trivia questions. Questions from Trivial Pursuit could be used instead.
2. Read each question aloud and instruct students to write their answers on a sheet of paper.
3. After students have completed their answers individually, divide the class into groups.
4. Read the questions aloud again. After each question, allow members to confer with each other to develop group answers.
5. After the groups have answered all of the questions, announce the correct answers.
6. Instruct group members to compare their individual answers to the group answers.

TEACHING TIPS

Instead of asking trivia questions, consider asking questions related to small group communication. Some of the multiple choice items provided in this instructor's resource manual could be used. Another alternative is to allow teams to compete against each other as they answer the questions. Competition can often be a motivator and generate more enthusiasm for the activity. Discussion questions:

❖ Generally, which set of answers were more accurate, the individual's or the group's?
❖ How important is it for everyone to be able to contribute information to a group?
❖ What are the advantages of pooling members' knowledge in a group?

CHAPTER 12

INFORMED GROUPS

NAME THAT SOURCE

GOALS

- To recognize different types of information.
- To apply tests of validity to information used in groups.

PARTICIPANTS

Groups of 4 to 6 members

PROCEDURE

1. Distribute copies of the *Is TV to Blame for Violence?* worksheet.
2. Instruct the groups to identify the type of information represented in each excerpt. For example, is it an example, testimony, a statistic, etc.?
3. Groups should then evaluate the quality of the information using the following criteria:
   - source qualification
   - recency
   - consistency
   - statistical validity
   - quantity

TEACHING TIPS

In this activity, the correct identification of information type is not as important as students' questions about the validity of the information. As an alternative, the instructor can supply excerpts from a local or campus newspaper. Discussion questions:

- ❖ How well did groups identify the type of each piece of information?
- ❖ What were the groups' conclusions regarding the validity of each piece of information?
- ❖ What was the most difficult part of evaluating the information?
- ❖ Why is it important for groups to evaluate the information they use to make decisions?

IS TV TO BLAME FOR VIOLENCE?

1. Television sets were found in fewer than 15 percent of America's homes in 1950. They were found in 93 percent of our homes in 1990. In that period, the number of murders per year in the United States increased from 7,942 to 21,860; the murder rate per 100,000 population approximately doubled—from 5.3 to 10.2. Television obviously contributed to the rise in crime.

   Type of Information:

   Validity of Information:

2. Brandon Centerwall of the University of Washington reports that "In the minds of young children, television is a source of entirely faulty information . . . [about] how the world works . . . . An Indiana school board had to issue an advisory to young children that . . . there is no such thing as Teenage Mutant Ninja Turtles. Children had been crawling down storm drains looking for them."

   Type of Information:

   Validity of Information:

3. The television industry . . . has claimed—legitimately, I suspect—that by exposing Americans to the racial violence and brutality inflicted on blacks in the South, the civil rights movement was advanced significantly.

   Type of Information:

   Validity of Information:

CHAPTER 12

INFORMED GROUPS

DO AS I SAY

GOAL

- To alert students to the importance of carefully reading materials when they are researching.

PARTICIPANTS

Entire class

PROCEDURE

1. Give all students a copy of the *Do as I Say* handout. Instruct them to not turn over the paper until it is time to begin.
2. Tell students they will have 3 minutes to complete following the directions.

TEACHING TIPS

Most students will not actually read the entire list before beginning their task. They will skip the critical instruction in the first line and move through the meaningless parts of the instructions. This can begin a discussion of the different problems encountered in the attempt to separate valuable and nonvaluable information while researching. This exercise can also be used to make general observations regarding the educational implications for matters such as test taking, preparation of papers, etc. Discussion questions:

- ❖ Why did you overlook the critical information in the first sentence?
- ❖ What factors can cause you to overlook the critical information and concentrate on less significant factors while researching?
- ❖ Did the time pressure affect your ability to follow directions?
- ❖ Did the fact that others were responding out loud reinforce your belief that you were following directions? Did the fact that some students seemed to be silent affect your belief that you were following directions?
- ❖ For those who did complete the assignment properly, what led you to follow the directions?

DO AS I SAY

1. Read this list completely before doing anything.
2. Work as rapidly as you can.
3. Put your name in the upper right hand corner of this paper.
4. Circle the word "name" in sentence three.
5. Underline the words "upper right hand" in sentence three.
6. Draw a circle around the title of this paper.
7. Call out your first name.
8. In sentence five, draw a circle around the word "underline."
9. Write down the name of your state's capital.
10. Underline all of sentence seven.
11. Humm a few bars of the National Anthem.
12. Draw an X in the lower left-hand corner of this paper.
13. Write the name of the city you live in.
14. Draw a circle around the word "capital" in sentence nine.
15. If you have followed instructions to this point, call out loud, "I have."
16. Close your eyes and raise your left hand over your head for a moment.
17. Draw four circles in the lower right-hand corner of this paper.
18. Count from ten to one backwards out loud in your normal speaking voice.
19. Do only what is asked of you in sentences one and twenty.
20. Do not give this test away. Remain silent but appear to be working.

CHAPTER 13

TECHNOLOGY AND VIRTUAL GROUPS

COMPUTER AND TELECONFERENCE SIMULATION

GOAL

- To demonstrate the advantages and disadvantages of computer conferencing and teleconferences.

PARTICIPANTS

Four groups of at least three members

PROCEDURE

This exercise is provided in the Groupwork section of the chapter.

1. Instruct group #1 to simulate teleconferencing. The group members will sit with their backs to each other and communicate orally. Group members should not look at each other.
2. Instruct group #2 to simulate synchronous computer conferencing. The group members will sit with their backs to each other and communicate by writing messages on index cards. Group members are encouraged to send messages whenever they choose. Messages should be passed to all members of the group and can be passed to the left or right. Group members should not look at each other.
3. Instruct group #3 to simulate an asynchronous computer conference. Group members will sit with their backs to each other and communicate by writing on a piece of paper. One individual will start the conference by writing an initial message. The paper will be passed to the left. The next group member will respond by writing a message on the same piece of paper and then will pass the paper to the left. The process continues in this fashion. Group members should not look at each other.
4. Instruct group #4 to engage in a face-to-face discussion.
5. Each group is to solve the following puzzle: Your group has eight balls, one of which is slightly heavier than the others. Your group also has a balance scale, which may be used only twice. Devise a method of finding the heavier ball.
6. After the simulations are complete, announce the answer to the puzzle to the class.

ANSWER TO THE PUZZLE:

Place three balls on each side of the balance scale (six total). (1) If the balance is even, the heavier ball is one of the two balls that has not been weighed. Weighing those two balls will show which is heavier. (2) If the balance is uneven, take the three balls from the heavier side of the scale. Weigh two of the three balls. If the scale balances, the heavier ball is the one that was not weighed. If the scale does not balance, the identity of the heavier ball will be disclosed.

TEACHING TIPS

This activity provides a good alternative to demonstrating the nature of each type of conference when it is not possible to gain access to the equipment required to conduct a computer or teleconference. Discussion questions:

- How did the conference method help or hinder resolution of the puzzle?
- Would the conference method be better suited to other types of tasks?
- What communication problems did the conference method create? Can they be resolved?
- Did the group members work as a group or individually?

CHAPTER 13

TECHNOLOGY AND VIRTUAL GROUPS

I WANT TO BE A TELECOMMUTER

GOAL

- To have students consider the implications of reliance on technology in the workplace.

PARTICIPANTS

Groups of 5 to 6 members

PROCEDURE

1. Divide the class into groups of 5 to 6 people. Tell them they have been selected for a job in which all their work is done by telecommuting.
2. Have the students generate a list of both the advantages and disadvantages of a telecommuting job. Tell them they should consider it from the perspective of both the employee and the employer.
3. Ask them to decide whether the advantages outweigh the disadvantages or vice versa.
4. A spokesperson should present each group's findings and conclusions to the class.

TEACHING TIPS

While few people will probably end up doing all their work by telecommuting in the near future, discussion of the topic permeates the media. Students should give consideration to all the ramifications of a reliance on telecommuting. Discussion questions:

- ❖ Did your group raise any advantages or disadvantages you had not thought of?
- ❖ Is there a difference between task-oriented and maintenance-oriented group functions with respect to telecommuting?
- ❖ Who do you believe benefits the most from telecommuting, employers or employees? Why?
- ❖ Would you consider accepting a telecommuting job? Why or Why not?

CHAPTER 13

TECHNOLOGY AND VIRTUAL GROUPS

TECHS AND THE CAMPUS

GOAL

- To make students more aware of the variety of technological changes that are having an impact on the educational environment.

PARTICIPANTS

Groups of 5 to 6 members

PROCEDURE

1. Divide the students into groups of 5 to 6 people. If possible, try to place at least one student who has taken an online course in each group.
2. Have students share their experiences with using technology during their educational careers. Some may have taken an on-line course, some may have used technology to prepare materials, many will have emailed instructors or other students, and most will have done research using the Internet.
3. Have the students generate a list of the advantages and disadvantages of each type of technology in terms of its impact on communication.
4. A spokesperson from each group should present the conclusions to the class.

TEACHING TIPS

Technology is having a major impact on the educational process but many students take its role for granted. This exercise asks students to reflect upon the specific impact of different technological tools. Discussion questions:

- What are the advantages and disadvantages of taking on-line courses?
- Are on-line courses better suited to some subjects than others? If so, which ones? Why?
- Would you consider taking an on-line course? Why or why not?
- Has the use of email increased your extent of communication with instructors? With other students? Why or why not?
- How extensively do you rely on the Internet for research?
- Are there any drawbacks to relying on the Internet for research?
- Do you believe reliance on Internet research contributes to plagiarism?

CHAPTER 14

PLANNING AND CONDUCTING MEETINGS

MEET THE PEOPLE PROBLEMS

GOAL

- To understand the principles and apply textbook suggestions to some of the common people problems that arise during meetings.

PARTICIPANTS

Groups of 5 to 7 members

PROCEDURE

This exercise is provided in the Groupwork section of the chapter.

1. Ask students to read the descriptions of additional people problems at the end of Chapter 14 or distribute the *People Problems* handout.
2. Instruct the groups to prepare at least two strategies for dealing with each type of people problem.
3. Groups should share their strategies with the entire class.

TEACHING TIPS

Groups can also discuss strategies for dealing with other types of disruptive members described in the text. Discussion questions:

❖ What general, over-riding principles emerge as effective strategies for dealing with difficult members?
❖ Which problems do you think are the most difficult to deal with?
❖ What might happen in a group that allows these problems to continue?

PEOPLE PROBLEMS

THE BROKEN RECORD

Brings up the same point or idea over and over again. Regardless of what other members say, the broken record keeps "singing the same song."

THE HEADSHAKER

Nonverbally responds in a disruptive manner. Shakes head, rolls eyes, groans, slams books shut, madly scribbles notes after someone has said something. Members begin reacting to what the headshaker does rather than what is said.

THE KNOW-IT-ALL

Uses age, seniority, credentials, and experience to argue a point. Know-It-Alls declare "I've been here for 20 years and I know this won't work," or "I'm the only one here with an accounting degree, so you'd better listen."

THE BACKSEAT DRIVER

Keeps telling everyone what they should do or should have done. "If we'd met earlier this week, we could have avoided this problem," or "I would have let everyone read the report rather than summarizing it."

THE ATTACKER

Launches personal attacks on other group members or the chairperson. Purposely zeros in on and criticizes the ideas and opinions of others.

CHAPTER 14

PLANNING AND CONDUCTING MEETINGS

WE HAVE TO STOP MEETING LIKE THIS

GOALS

- To identify the causes of ineffective group meetings.
- To find solutions to common meeting problems.

PARTICIPANTS

Groups of 4 to 7 members (This activity can also be done as an entire class.)

PROCEDURE

1. Divide the class into groups.
2. Ask students to recall some of the ineffective or frustrating meetings that they have attended in the past.
3. Instruct the groups to brainstorm and record as many responses as possible to the following question: "What do I dislike about meetings?" The brainstorming session should last approximately 10 minutes.
4. After brainstorming, ask the groups to develop at least five strategies that meeting planners and participants can employ to improve the quality of meetings.
5. Each group should select a spokesperson to present its strategies to the entire class.

TEACHING TIPS

It may be helpful to introduce the guidelines for brainstorming explained in Chapter 9 of the textbook. If possible, have the groups record their answers on the chalkboard. This makes all of the lists easy to reference during the class discussion. Follow the brainstorming session with a discussion of the importance of carefully planned meetings. Discussion questions:

- What were some of the problems that almost all of the groups included on their lists?
- Are most of the meetings you attend productive and pleasant experiences?
- Do you think most meetings are worthwhile? Why or why not?
- What is the likelihood that you will have to attend regular meetings in your chosen profession?

CHAPTER 14

PLANNING AND CONDUCTING MEETINGS

PLANNING A MEETING

GOAL

- To demonstrate the guidelines of meeting planning.

PARTICIPANTS

Groups of 4 to 6 members

PROCEDURE

1. Present the following situation to the groups:

   The college has just announced that it is considering a significant increase in tuition in order to maintain the current services offered to students. Not surprisingly, the students are opposed to a tuition increase. The members of your group have been selected to represent the student body in a meeting with college officials. Your group has requested the meeting and is responsible for planning it.

2. The groups should begin by determining what they want to accomplish during a meeting with college officials.
3. Instruct the groups to plan the meeting by answering the following questions:
   - Who should attend the meeting?
   - When should the meeting take place?
   - Where should the meeting occur?
   - What materials will be needed at the meeting?
4. After answering all of the questions, each group should appoint one of its members to act as the meeting's chairperson.
5. Each chairperson should briefly present the group's answers to the entire class.

TEACHING TIPS

This activity works best when students are familiar with the meeting planning guidelines suggested in the textbook. Discussion questions:

- ❖ How difficult was it to plan the meeting?
- ❖ Which question was the most difficult to answer?
- ❖ What could happen during this hypothetical meeting if it is not well planned?
- ❖ On what basis did each group select its chairperson? Did that person demonstrate qualities during the discussion that would make him or her an effective chairperson?

CHAPTER 14

PLANNING AND CONDUCTING MEETINGS

CREATING AN AGENDA

GOALS

- To create a meeting agenda.
- To understand the decisions that must be made when preparing an agenda.

PARTICIPANTS

Groups of 5 to 8 members

PROCEDURE

1. Inform the students that they are members of a committee created to address the rise of crime in a neighborhood.
2. Distribute copies of the *Community Crime Committee* handout.
3. Instruct the groups to develop an agenda for the committee's next meeting based on the information in the handout.
4. Each group selects a meeting chairperson.
5. After the agendas have been completed, instruct the chairperson to present the group's agenda to the entire class.

TEACHING TIPS

This activity should follow a review of the basic elements included in the traditional business agenda discussed in the textbook. Instead of using the hypothetical case provided, students working on graded group projects could develop an agenda for their next group meeting. Discussion questions:

- ❖ What were some of the major differences among the groups' agendas?
- ❖ What were some of the more difficult decisions you had to make in preparing the agenda?
- ❖ How important is preparing an agenda for a meeting?
- ❖ Now that the agenda has been prepared, what are the responsibilities of the meeting's chairperson?
- ❖ Once they receive the agenda, what are the responsibilities of the group members?

COMMUNITY CRIME COMMITTEE

You are a member of a committee established by your city's mayor to address the rise in crime in the community. During the group's first meeting, members became acquainted and discussed the recent increase of crime in the neighborhood. One of the members agreed to get crime reports from the local police precinct and present the information at the next meeting. Another member was asked to find out what secretarial assistance the committee could request from the mayor's office.

The group began discussing a proposed town hall meeting between citizens and local law enforcement officials. There was not enough time during the committee's first meeting to complete the plans for the town hall meeting. At the second meeting, the group also wants to discuss ways of encouraging more community involvement, a plan for patrolling the playground, and other methods of reducing the spread of crime.

CHAPTER 14

MEETINGS PLANNING AND CONDUCTING

WHAT DO THE MINUTES REVEAL?

GOALS

- To understand the differences between formal and informal minutes.
- To review the types of information that should be found in formal minutes.

PARTICIPANTS

Groups of 4 to 6 members

PROCEDURE

1. Before class, obtain copies of the minutes from your college's Board of Trustees meeting.
2. Distribute the minutes to groups. Allow them sufficient time to become familiar with the document before beginning the group discussions.
3. Instruct the groups to evaluate the minutes using the guidelines for preparing agenda and minutes in Chapter 14.

TEACHING TIPS

This activity works best after students are familiar with the purpose and elements of a meeting's agenda and minutes. Copies of another group's formal minutes could be used for this activity. You may prefer to have groups evaluate the formal meeting minutes of a school board, a city council, or the student government association. If you have time, you may wish to have students compare and contrast two sets of minutes. Discussion questions:

- Who was the meeting's recorder? Was the recorder a member of the group?
- Do the minutes reveal the formality of the meeting? How formal are this group's meetings?
- Did the document contain all of the essential elements of good minutes?
- Do the minutes appear objective?
- Did the physical and linguistic composition of the minutes cause you to form any impression of the group?
- Assuming that you did not attend the meeting, how understandable were the minutes?

CHAPTER 14

PLANNING AND CONDUCTING MEETINGS

DESIGNING AN AGENDA FORM

GOALS

- To highlight the essential elements in a meeting agenda.
- To create a useful agenda form for future meetings.

PARTICIPANTS

Groups of 5 to 7 members

PROCEDURE

1. Instruct the groups to use the textbook's list of essential elements and additional options for an agenda to create an original, standardized agenda form.
2. Urge groups to make sure that their fill-in-the-blank agenda form reminds them of things that should be noted or covered before, during, and after a meeting.
3. Explain that in addition to the topics for discussion and action, the agenda should include items and information that help group members prepare and participate effectively. Examples: names of participants, invited guests, material needed for the meeting, action item assignments and deadlines, time allocated for discussion or action, scheduled oral presentations, etc.

TEACHING TIPS

The class should be familiar with the essential elements of an agenda before beginning this assignment. Encourage the groups to type and make copies of their forms for use in their own group meetings as they prepare for graded group projects. Discussion questions:

- ❖ Which elements might be overlooked if you were not using such a form?
- ❖ Does your form include all of the essential elements of an agenda?
- ❖ Could your form be used by most groups? Why or why not?

CHAPTER 15

MAKING PRESENTATIONS IN GROUPS

A PRACTICE SPEECH

GOALS

- To practice delivery skills.
- To provide experience in impromptu, extemporaneous, manuscript, and memorized speaking.

PARTICIPANTS

All members of the class

PROCEDURE

This exercise is provided in the Groupwork section of the chapter.

1. Each student should prepare a short oral presentation in which four forms of delivery are used as follows:
   - Memorized: Recite 30 seconds of something memorized—a poem, the Pledge of Allegiance, song lyrics, etc.
   - Manuscript: Read 60 seconds of any piece of prose—a book, a newspaper or magazine article, etc.
   - Extemporaneous: Spend 60 seconds talking to the audience about a personal experience or opinion—what hobbies you have, what you think about a campus or political issue, etc.
   - Impromptu: After completing the above presentations, someone in the audience should ask a question. Answer the question in 30 seconds or less.
2. Listeners should use the *Delivery Checklist* to assess each speaker's performance.

TEACHING TIPS

The activity works well as a follow-up to a discussion of performance and oral presentations. Discussion questions:

- ❖ Which forms of delivery were the most natural?
- ❖ Which forms had the most eye contact?
- ❖ Which forms were the most interesting to look at?
- ❖ Which forms were the easiest to listen to?
- ❖ What problems arose in each of the forms? Were they unique to the form or universal?
- ❖ What general conclusions can you draw from this experience?

DELIVERY CHECKLIST

Does the speaker . . .

__________ take time and get set before beginning the presentation?

__________ establish eye contact before beginning?

__________ begin without referring to notes?

__________ maintain eye contact for most of the presentation?

__________ gesture and move naturally?

__________ avoid distracting movements?

__________ speak with adequate volume?

__________ articulate clearly?

__________ pronounce words correctly?

__________ respond and adjust to feedback?

CHAPTER 15

MAKING PRESENTATIONS IN GROUPS

COMMON GROUND

GOALS

- To understand the importance of finding common ground when a topic is controversial and/or when listeners disagree with the group.
- To help students identify a belief or behavior they share with listeners.

PARTICIPANTS

Groups of 3 to 5 members

PROCEDURE

1. Review the concept of common ground with the class.
2. Instruct the groups to identify common ground by completing the following statements:
   - Pro-life and pro-choice advocates would probably agree that . . .
   - Those who want to cap doctors' fees and those who oppose such caps would probably agree that . . .
   - Vegetarians and meat-eaters would probably agree that . . .
   - Animal rights activists and those who support the use of animals in medical experimentation would probably agree that . . .
   - Affirmative action advocates and affirmative action opponents would probably agree that . . .
3. Each group should select a spokesperson to present its answers to the class.

TEACHING TIPS

Other current political and social issues can be substituted for the statements provided above. Follow the activity with a discussion of the purpose of identifying common ground with listeners. Discussion questions:

❖ How difficult was it to identify common ground for each statement?
❖ How can common ground be used when preparing an oral presentation?
❖ What other strategies could be used to deal with hostile listeners?

CHAPTER 15

MAKING PRESENTATIONS IN GROUPS

CHOOSING VISUAL AIDS

GOALS

- To understand that different kinds of presentation topics call for different types of visual aids.
- To understand the potential uses and limits of the different types of visual aids.

PARTICIPANTS

Groups of 4 to 6 members.

PROCEDURE

1. Discuss the different types of visual aids available to speakers during an oral presentation.
2. Instruct the groups to list three different visual aids that could be used to support the following oral presentations:
   - Purpose: To explain the college's plans for a new building.
   - Purpose: To describe methods of time management.
   - Purpose: To persuade listeners to participate in a blood drive.
3. Each group should select a spokesperson to present the suggested visual aids.

TEACHING TIPS

Encourage students to be creative as they think of possible visual aids. Follow the activity with a discussion of the uses and options for visual aids. Discussion questions:

- ❖ How would visual aids enhance the oral presentations?
- ❖ What are the consequences of using a poorly prepared visual aid during an oral presentation?
- ❖ What are some of the things that can go wrong when presenters use visual aids? How can those problems be prevented?

CHAPTER 15

MAKING PRESENTATIONS IN GROUPS

SHOW ME THE SLIDES

GOAL

- To develop an appropriate presentation aid using computer software.

PARTICIPANTS

Groups of 3 members (this activity can also be assigned to the entire class to be completed individually).

PROCEDURE

1. Instruct students to review Chapter 15 and choose a section or concept to illustrate on an overhead transparency or computer slide.
2. Students are to actually create a slide using any presentation software available to them. Students usually have no problem using either a group member's computer or equipment in a computer lab.
3. Remind students to follow the guidelines presented in Chapter 15 for developing visual aids and using technology.
4. During the next class session, groups are to display their overheads or slides (depending on the available equipment) to the class.
5. The entire class should critique each presentation aid and comment on the strengths and weaknesses of each.

TEACHING TIPS

Another option is to have groups also develop an example of a poorly created presentation aid violating as many guidelines as possible. Discussion questions:

- ❖ Do any of the presentation aids use too many colors, fonts, etc.?
- ❖ Are the typefaces readable?
- ❖ Is there any unnecessary artwork?
- ❖ Do any of the slides use a multimedia effect? Was it appropriate?
- ❖ Have copyright laws been violated?
- ❖ What are the strengths of each presentation aid?
- ❖ How could each presentation aid be improved?
- ❖ What were some of the decisions that were made when developing the presentation aid?
- ❖ What difficulties were encountered in developing the presentation aid?

APPENDIX

PARLIAMENTARY PROCEDURE

THE MASCOT DEBATE

GOAL

- To provide groups with experience using parliamentary procedure.

PARTICIPANTS

Four equally sized groups

PROCEDURE

This exercise is provided in the Groupwork section of the chapter.

1. Inform students that an assembly has been called to debate the following motion: The college's mascot should be changed from the _____________ (fill in the college's current mascot) to the _______________ (fill in another animal or character as the mascot).
2. Each group is to advocate a separate position on the motion.
   - Group #1: The mascot should be changed to _______________
   - Group #2: The mascot should not be changed and should remain as is.
   - Group #3: The motion should be amended to _______________ (add a specific characteristic to the mascot-for example, a *blue and gold* buffalo, a *fighting* fish).
   - Group #4: Members are free to advocate any of the above positions.
3. Permit each group a short period of time to discuss its position on the motion and develop a strategy to achieve its goal.
4. The instructor will serve as chair or appoint a member of the assembly to act as chair.
5. The assembly must debate and vote on the motion.

TEACHING TIPS

Encourage students to use as many of the common motions as they wish throughout the activities. Consider distributing or displaying the common motions summarized in the textbook on an overhead projector. Discussion questions:

- ❖ Which motions were the most confusing?
- ❖ Which motions were the most valuable in maintaining an orderly discussion?
- ❖ How difficult was it to keep track of the amendments during the debate?

APPENDIX

PARLIAMENTARY PROCEDURE

I MOVE THAT . . .

GOALS

- To practice using parliamentary procedure to conduct a group discussion.
- To practice argumentation skills in a group.

PARTICIPANTS

The entire class

PROCEDURE

1. Review the basic rules for using parliamentary procedure.
2. Inform students that the entire class will participate in a debate using parliamentary procedure. They are encouraged to use as many of the types of motions as possible during the debate.
3. The instructor will chair the debate.
4. The class is to debate the issue of euthanasia and/or physician-assisted suicide.

TEACHING TIPS

The instructor may choose any controversial issue for the debate. It may be helpful to distribute or display on an overhead projector a copy of the common motions. Encourage students to use a variety of motions. Another alternative is to let students chair the debate. To provide several students with the opportunity to chair, assign a different student to the role every five minutes throughout the debate. It is not necessary that the debate come to a vote, though you might want to encourage the class to call the question when you are ready to move to a class discussion of the activity. Discussion questions:

❖ What was the most difficult part of using parliamentary procedure?
❖ In what types of group situations would parliamentary procedure be valuable?
❖ Is it necessary for all groups to use all of the formal rules? Why or why not?
❖ Which rules do you think are the most useful to groups?
❖ If student chairs were used, how comfortable were they while presiding? How comfortable did they seem to be?

APPENDIX

PARLIAMENTARY PROCEDURE

GOVERNMENT IN ACTION

GOALS

- To observe the use of parliamentary procedure by legislative groups.
- To understand the principles of parliamentary procedure.

PARTICIPANTS

The entire class

PROCEDURE

1. Before class, obtain a video recording of the U.S. Congress or a local government meeting.
2. Review the basic principles and rules for parliamentary procedure.
3. Have the class watch a portion of the video recording.
4. Follow the video with a class discussion of the uses of parliamentary procedure.

TEACHING TIPS

If you do not have access to cable yourself, a media resource center on your campus may be able to provide you with a CSPAN broadcast of the U.S. Congress. Local government meetings often appear on cable television. Try to use a segment that shows members using several of the rules. Discussion questions:

❖ What parts of the procedure were most confusing?
❖ How do the rules provide everyone with an equal opportunity to participate?
❖ What might happen during such meetings in the absence of formal rules?
❖ How do the rules promote an orderly discussion?

APPENDIX

PARLIAMENTARY PROCEDURE

HEAR, HEAR

GOALS

- To observe the use of parliamentary procedure by a legislative group.
- To observe cultural differences in the use of parliamentary procedure and argumentation.

PARTICIPANTS

Entire class

PROCEDURE

1. Before class, obtain a video recording of the British Parliament. CSPAN usually airs excerpts of Prime Minister's Question Time each week.
2. Discuss with students how Parliamentary Procedure began with the British but that there are differences between how the U.S. and Britian engage in debate in their legislatures.
3. Have the class watch a portion of the video recording.
4. Follow the airing with a discussion of the procedures used by the British.

TEACHING TIPS

If you do not have access to cable on your own, your campus media center may be able to assist you. This exercise allows you to discuss how certain accepted rules of procedure are essentially culturally determined. The exercise works best if you have also used the exercise that has students viewing a session of the U.S. Congress.
Discussion questions:

- ❖ What were the major similarities between the U.S. and British legislatures? What were the major differences?
- ❖ Did you find any of the actions in the British House of Commons particularly problematic? Did you find any that you wish the U.S. Congress would adopt?
- ❖ Do you think the British system would work in the U.S.? Why or why not?
- ❖ Can you draw any conclusions about the impact of culture on the determination of rules and norms?

APPENDIX

PARLIAMENTARY PROCEDURE

WHO WANTS TO BE A PARLIAMENTARIAN?

GOAL

- To learn and apply the basic rules of parliamentary procedure.

PARTICIPANTS

Groups of 3 to 5 members

PROCEDURE

1. Tell each group to prepare a set of 15 quiz questions (and their answers) regarding the rules of parliamentary procedure. This may be done in advance of the class day on which the exercise is conducted. Each question and answer should be written on a 3 x 5 card.

    Examples:
    Name three ways in which a motion can be amended.
    Which motion has a higher precedent: A motion to adjourn or amend?
    What motion would you use to find out the proper procedure to make a motion?
    True or false: The chair can take an active part in the meeting and voice his or her views at any time.
    When can the chair vote?
2. The instructor collects all the questions.
3. Each group chooses a "champion" to play the game. The instructor acts as quiz master and asks a question of each champion in turn. When champions cannot answer the question or answers a question incorrectly, they are "out" of the game.
4. Champions may use two lifelines to their group during the game. They may ask the group to answer the question and then decide whether to use the answer. By the end of the game or time period, the winner or winners are declared.

TEACHING TIPS

Who Wants to Be a Parliamentarian? is, of course, modeled after Who Wants to Be a Millionaire? You can keep this game simple or embellish it with all the trappings of the television show. If you are not comfortable serving as quiz master, a dramatic student may want to take on the role with all its suspense as well as its famous line, "Is that your final answer?" If you want to make parliamentary procedure into a bigger unit, you can expand the number of rules beyond those presented in the textbook. Depending on how you want to play the game, you can also offer prizes to the winners, the champions, and the winning group.

Test Bank

Chapter 1
Introduction to Small Group Communication

Multiple Choice

1. Which of the following situations best represents small group communication as defined in the textbook?
   a. People talking in an elevator.
   b. People discussing the weather at an airport.
   c. Fans cheering at a baseball game.
Δ d. Jury members deliberating a court case.
   e. A congregation listening to a sermon.

2. Synergy occurs when
   a. all members participate equally.
   b. the group reaches an agreement.
Δ c. the knowledge, talents and dedication of group members merge.
   d. the group accomplishes its task.
   e. the group selects its leader.

3. What is the ideal group size for a problem-solving discussion?
   a. 3-5 people
   b. 4-6 people
Δ c. 5-7 people
   d. 6-8 people
   e. 7-9 people

4. The cooperative interaction of several factors that results in a combined effect greater than the total of all individual parts is referred to as
   a. interaction.
   b. common goals.
   c. interdependence.
Δ d. synergy.
   e. working.

5. According to your textbook, approximately how many meetings occur daily in the United States?
   a. 1 million
   b. 5 million
   c. 9 million
Δ d. 11 million
   e. 15 million

6. A virtual group is one which

Δ a. relies on technology to communicate.
b. exists only for a short period of time.
c. lacks a leader.
d. lacks a clear purpose.
e. has the same dynamic as other groups.

7. A stamp collecting club is an example a

a. self-help group.
Δ b. social group.
c. learning group.
b. service group.
e. public group.

8. The local Parents Without Partners chapter in a community is an example of a

Δ a. self-help group.
b. social group.
c. learning group.
d. service group.
e. public group.

9. A community establishes an awards committee that disbands once it has completed the task of choosing employees to be honored at the annual awards dinner. The awards committee is an example of

a. a standing committee.
Δ b. an *ad hoc* committee.
c. a task force.
d. a symposium.
e. a self-management team.

10. A civic association's ongoing finance committee is an example of

Δ a. a standing committee.
b. an *ad hoc* committee.
c. a task force.
d. a symposium.
e. a forum.

11. A __________ is a small number of people with complementary skills who are committed to a common purpose, performance goals, and an approach to work for which they hold themselves mutually accountable.

a. self-help group
b. synergistic group
c. learning group
Δ d. self-management team
e. task force

12. Guests who appear on talk shows and interact with other guests for the benefit of an audience are participating in a
    a. symposium.
    b. forum.
Δ   c. panel discussion.
    d. governance group.
    e. service group.

13. A group of police officers presenting short, uninterrupted speeches on different aspects of community safety are participating in a
Δ   a. symposium.
    b. forum.
    c. panel discussion.
    d. governance group.
    e. self-help group.

14. A college appoints a moderator and holds an open discussion to provide students with the opportunity to ask questions and express their concerns regarding a proposed increase in tuition. This setting for group communication is an example of a
    a. symposium.
Δ   b. forum.
    c. panel discussion.
    d. governance group.
    e. service group.

15. A college's Board of Trustees that makes public policy decisions may be classified as a
    a. symposium.
    b. forum.
    c. panel discussion.
Δ   d. governance group.
    e. service group.

16. Statements that explain or predict how groups work are
Δ   a. theories.
    b. methods.
    c. tools.
    d. synergistic.
    e. balanced.

17. Noise in a group may be defined as
    a. too many people talking at once.
    b. a radio blasting in the background.
    c. an uncomfortable physical setting.
Δ   d. anything that interferes with communication.
    e. members who are consistently late and loud in entering the room.

18. The purpose or objective toward which a group is directed is referred to as
    a. interaction.
    b. synergy.
Δ c. a common goal.
    d. interdependence
    e. small group communication.

19. Collaborative learning promotes higher individual achievement in
    a. retention.
    b. knowledge acquisition.
    c. accuracy.
    d. creativity in problem solving.
Δ e. All of the above.

20. Your family members would best be considered which type of group?
Δ a. Primary group
    b. Social group
    c. Public group
    d. Service group
    e. None of the above.

True/False

1. Business experts suggest that, in the future, self-management teams will surpass individuals as the primary performance unit in American companies.
   Answer: True

2. According to a study by Larson and LaFasto, interdependence is the single factor that separates successful groups from unsuccessful groups.
   Answer: False

3. Employers view proficiency in a field of study as more important than group-related skills.
   Answer: False

4. Theories are guidelines, procedures, techniques, and skills for dealing with issues and problems that arise within groups.
   Answer: False

5. The key to balancing both the complex and competing elements in a group is a commitment to working toward the group's goal.
   Answer: True

6. As groups grow larger individual member satisfaction increases.
   Answer: False

7. Groups always perform better than individuals working alone.
   Answer: False

8. Individuals tend to learn more when working within groups rather than working alone.
   Answer: True

9. A group is in balance once it has achieved its assigned task.
   Answer: False

10. The ideal size of a small group is three to four members.
   Answer: False

Essay

1. Hawkins and Fillion surveyed personnel directors to find which skills were most important for successful group participation. Discuss five of those skills.

2. Your textbook's definition of small group communication consists of six essential elements. Identify and explain the importance of each element of the definition.

3. Discuss the concept of synergy. Include in your discussion both a definition of synergy and an indication of the role it plays in group communication.

4. There are both advantages and disadvantages to working in groups. List and explain three advantages of working in groups. List and explain three disadvantages of working in groups.

5. Your textbook authors claim that communication is the medium through which groupwork is done. Explain what they mean by this statement. Do you agree with this statement? Why or why not?

6. Your textbook claims that experiential learning helps students learn the skills that are necessary for working in groups. What is experiential learning? How does it promote the acquisition of skills?

7. Define and distinguish between the concepts of synchronous and asynchronous groups. Include in your answer an example of each.

8. Define and distinguish between the two types of noises discussed in the textbook.

9. Discuss the concept of a "self-management team." Include in your answer an indication of the role such teams play in the work environment.

10. Discuss the concept of balance in a group. Include in your answer an explanation of the major factors necessary to achieve balance.

Chapter 2
Group Formation and Development

Multiple Choice

1. Affiliating with a circle of friends because you want to be liked by and feel part of a group can satisfy which of Maslow's Hierarchy of Needs?
   a. Safety
   b. Self-actualization
   c. Physiological
   d. Esteem
   Δ e. Belongingness

2. Members interested in satisfying the esteem needs of other group members should
   a. establish subgroups designed to safeguard members from danger or harm.
   b. be realistic, independent, and confident.
   c. work to provide basic group needs such as shelter from the cold or heat.
   d. create a group environment in which members feel liked.
   Δ e. reward group members for their contributions.

3. Joining a group because you believe it will make you a better person or help you realize more of your potential can fulfill which of Maslow's Hierarchy of Needs?
   a. Safety
   Δ b. Self-actualization
   c. Physiological
   d. Esteem
   e. Belongingness

4. Which of the following terms describes a member who tends to withdraw from the group and avoids active participation because his or her inclusion needs have not been met?
   Δ a. Undersocial member
   b. Abdicrat
   c. Autocrat
   d. Oversocial member
   e. Overpersonal member

5. _____________ want control in groups but are reluctant to pursue it. They are often submissive members because they have no hope of having any control in the group. They will do what they are told and avoid responsibilities.
   a. Autocrats
   Δ b. Abdicrats
   c. Underpersonal members
   d. Undersocial members
   e. Ideal personal members

6. A member who attempts to fulfill his or her control needs by dominating the group is an
   a. undersocial member.
   b. abdicrat.
   Δ c. autocrat.
   d. oversocial member.
   e. underpersonal member.

7. __________ are aloof and uninvolved as a result of unmet affection needs.
   a. Overpersonal members
   b. Abdicrats
   c. Autocrats
   d. Undersocial members
   Δ e. Underpersonal members

8. You have just joined a newly formed group responsible for developing a recycling program for your community. At first group members are somewhat uncomfortable working with strangers. Which of Tuckman's stages of group development is your group experiencing?
   a. Norming
   Δ b. Forming
   c. Storming
   d. Performing
   e. Reforming

9. A neighborhood watch group formed to deter crime in the community is most likely fulfilling which of Maslow's Hierarchy of needs?
   Δ a. Safety
   b. Self-actualization
   c. Esteem
   d. Belongingness
   e. Physiological

10. Juries tend to
    a. progress sequentially through each of Tuckman's stages.
    Δ b. jump around on Tuckman's stages but fill each of them.
    c. skip the forming stage.
    d. skip the storming stage.
    e. skip the norming stage.

11. Control in a group refers to the
    a. individual holding an official leadership position.
    b. individual holding an unofficial leadership position.
    c. extent to which the meeting takes place on time.
    Δ d. extent to which members feel competent, confident, and free to make choices.
    e. extent to which meetings stay on the agenda.

12. In the _______________ phase of Fisher's group development phases, a search for solutions and decisions replaces arguments.
    a. orientation
    b. conflict
    Δ c. emergence
    d. reinforcement
    e. deviation

13. Your group has discussed and decided that members will take turns recording and typing the minutes from each meeting. A(n) _______________ has been established.
    a conforming norm
    b. implicit norm
    c. deviant norm
    Δ d. explicit norm
    e. inclusion norm

14. Whenever your department has a staff meeting, the supervisor always sits at the head of the table. Group members know they should not take the seat at the head of the table even though they have not been told. A(n) _______________ is operating in the group.
    a. conforming norm
    Δ b. implicit norm
    c. deviant norm
    d. explicit norm
    e. inclusion norm

15. Your group makes decisions by majority rule. A(n) _______________ is operating in this circumstance.
    a. status norm
    b. interaction norm
    c. achievement norm
    Δ d. procedural norm
    e. inclusion norm

16. Implicit norms are
    a. easy to recognize.
    b. quickly apparent to new members.
    Δ c. rarely discussed.
    d. imposed by an outside authority.
    e. disruptive of the group process.

17. According to Schutz, a group member who feels accepted by the group is an
    Δ a. ideal social member.
    b. undersocial member.
    c. ideal personal member.
    d. overpersonal member.
    e. underpersonal member.

18. Deviation from group norms or expections
    a. will always undermine group performance.
    Δ b. can improve group performance.
    c. occurs only when stubborn members are present.
    d. occurs under poor leadership.
    e. occurs only in the storming stage.

19. Which of the following factors can derail a group from an ideal sequence of group development phases?
    a. Group size
    b. Clarity of goals
    c. Availability of information
    d. Both b and c.
    Δ e. All of the above.

20. Changes in groups
    a. should be kept to a minimum.
    b. should always be avoided.
    c. should occur only in terms of group membership.
    Δ d. require difficult adjustments.
    e. should never involve norms.

True/False

1. Face-to-face meetings may be desirable in the early stages of virtual groups.
   Answer: True

2. An abdicrat is a group member whose control needs are met, who has no problem with power, and who is comfortable giving and taking orders.
   Answer: False

3. Tuckman's phases of group development include orientation, conflict, emergence, and reinforcement.
   Answer: False

4. Norms are sets of expectations concerning the kinds of behavior that are appropriate or inappropriate in a group.
   Answer: True

5. Destructive deviation occurs when a member resists a norm while still working to promote a group goal.
   Answer: False

6. Effective groups should strive for complete conformity to the group's norms.
   Answer: False

7. A new member to an established group should probably avoid disagreeing with members initially.
   Answer: True

8. All groups have interrelated task and social dimensions.
   Answer: True

9. Maslow's Hierarchy of Needs include inclusion, control, and affection.
   Answer: False

10. Explicit norms are more important than implicit norms.
    Answer: False

Essay

1. What are the differences between constructive and destructive deviation from group norms? Under what circumstances could deviation from group norms help group members work together to achieve a common goal?

2. Abraham Maslow ranks five critical human needs which may be satisfied by participation in groups. Identify all five needs in their proper order beginning with the most fundamental need. How can participation in groups satisfy each of these needs?

3. What is the difference between the task and social dimension of a group? What are the potential consequences of ignoring the task dimension of a group? What are the potential consequences of ignoring the social dimension of a group?

4. Discuss the concept of group norms. How can you use information about group norms to become a more effective member?

5. Identify the different group development stages identified by Tuckman and Fisher. What are the similarities and differences among the three models of group development? Which do you believe is the most descriptive of small groups? Explain your conclusion.

6. Identify the four categories of norms discussed in the textbook. Provide an example of each type of norm.

7. One of the challenges of working in groups is adapting to changing membership. How should a new group member behave when joining an already established group? How might a new group member go about learning the group's norms?

8. Discuss the factors of group formation that may be unique to virtual groups. Include in your answer an indication of the actions that might need to be altered in virtual groups.

9. Define and distinguish between explicit and implicit norms. Include in your answer an indication of the impact each type may have on new group members.

10. Discuss several of the ways in which group norms may be changed.

Chapter 3
Participation in Groups

Multiple Choice

1. ______________ functions primarily affect a group's ability to achieve its goals.
   a. Self-centered
   Δ b. Task
   c. Maintenance
   d. Participation
   e. All of the above.

2. ______________ group members get along with one another while pursuing a shared goal.
   a. Self-centered
   b. Task
   Δ c. Maintenance
   d. Participation
   e. All of the above.

3. ______________ functions describe negative roles in which individual needs are put ahead of both the group's goal and other members' needs.
   Δ a. Self-centered
   b. Task
   c. Maintenance
   d. Participation
   e. All of the above.

4. "I checked with our minority affairs officer and she said...." This statement would most likely be made by a group member functioning in which of the following task roles?
   a. Information seeker
   Δ b. Information giver
   c. Opinion seeker
   d. Opinion giver
   e. Clarifier-summarizer

5. "That's fine with me. Just tell me what to do." This statement would most likely be made by a group member functioning in which of the following roles?
   Δ a. Follower
   b. Deserter
   c. Harmonizer
   d. Blocker
   e. Tension releaser

6. "Maria, we haven't heard from you yet and want to make sure that everyone gets a chance to weigh in on this issue." This statement would most likely be made by a group member functioning in which of the following roles?
   a. Harmonizer
   b. Standard monitor
   c. Observer-interpreter
   Δ d. Gatekeeper
   e. Encourager-supporter

7. Richard contributes very little during meetings, frequently appears bored and disinterested in the group's work, and often leaves meetings early claiming he has a more important appointment. Richard could best be described as a
   Δ a. deserter.
   b. blocker.
   c. special interest pleader.
   d. dominator.
   e. aggressor.

8. Oscar is very outgoing and tends to talk more than others during group discussions. He enjoys working in the group and encourages others to get involved. Which Myers-Briggs® personality trait best describes Jasper?
   a. Thinker
   Δ b. Extrovert
   c. Feeler
   d. Introvert
   e. Sensor

9. Wanda tends to focus on details of the group project. She prefers to concentrate on one task at a time. Of all the group members, Wanda is the most likely to discover a flaw in an idea. Which Myers-Briggs® personality trait best describes Wanda?
   Δ a. Sensor
   b. Thinker
   c. Intuitive
   d. Perceiver
   e. Feeler

10. Kim is people-oriented. She wants everyone in the group to get along. She often spends extra time helping other group members. Which Myers-Briggs® personality trait best describes Kim?
    a. Sensor
    b. Thinker
    c. Intuitive
    d. Perceiver
    Δ e. Feeler

11. Dennis is always the most organized member of his group. He frequently encourages the group to plan ahead. He develops lengthy "To Do" lists of tasks for the group to follow. Which Myers-Briggs® personality trait best describes Dennis?
    a. Sensor
Δ b. Judger
    c. Intuitive
    d. Perceiver
    e. Thinker

12. Which of the following strategies is recommended as an effective method for dealing with deviant group members?
    a. Accept the deviant member's behavior.
    b. Confront the deviant and try to modify his or her behavior.
    c. Exclude the member by ignoring his or her comments during the discussion.
Δ d. All of the above.
    e. None of the above.

13. Even when everyone else in the group is upset or confused, Anthony stays cool, calm, and objective. He doesn't mind making tough decisions and can't understand why other group members get upset about things that are not relevant to the issue under discussion. In most situations, Anthony thinks it is more important to be right than liked. Which Myers-Briggs® personality trait best describes Anthony?
    a. Extrovert
    b. Sensor
    c. Intuitive
Δ d. Thinker
    e. Perceiver

14. Reggie is good at coordinating the group's work and keeping it organized. He never misses a deadline and expects others to do the same. Which Myers-Briggs® personality trait best describes Reggie?
    a. Sensor
Δ b. Judger
    c. Intuitive
    d. Perceiver
    e. Thinker

15. Jason appears to be a very private person. He carefully thinks about what he is going to say before speaking. He enjoys the group but would prefer to work alone. Which Myers-Briggs® personality trait best describes Jason?
    a. Extrovert
Δ b. Introvert
    c. Perceiver
    d. Judger
    e. None of the above.

16. Tawana is very good at seeing the big picture. However, when the group is discussing specific facts and details, she tends to get bored. Which Myers-Briggs® personality trait best describes Tawana?
    a. Sensor
    b. Feeler
    c. Thinker
    Δ d. Intuitive
    e. Perceiver

17. Stephanie dislikes deadlines and frequently doesn't complete her part of the group's task on time. Instead, she would prefer to go with the flow and be more spontaneous. Which Myers-Briggs® personality trait best describes Stephanie?
    a. Sensor
    b. Feeler
    c. Thinker
    d. Intuitive
    Δ e. Perceiver

18. Hidden agendas
    a. exist in every group.
    b. occur when there is poor leadership.
    c. always disrupt a group's functions.
    d. should always be confronted by a group.
    Δ e. do not necessarily cause problems in a group.

19. Exclusion from a group includes
    a. ignoring the group member.
    b. assigning the member an unimportant task.
    c. expelling the group member.
    Δ d. All of the above.
    e. None of the above.

20. In High Context cultures messages are
    Δ a. implicit.
    b. explicit.
    c. objective.
    d. factual.
    e. All of the above.

True/False

1. It is possible for one group member to function in several different roles at the same time.
   Answer: True

2. The ideal group would be composed of members who all represent the Myers-Briggs® personality type of extroverted thinker.
   Answer: False

3. An opinion seeker is fulfilling group maintenance roles.
   Answer: False
4. Apathy is indifference to a group and/or its goals.
   Answer: True
5. Sensor personalities in the Myers-Briggs® typology prefer to deal with details.
   Answer: False
6. The ideal group consists of each member fulfilling all of the task, maintenance, and self-centered roles.
   Answer: False
7. Hidden agendas always undermine a group's functionality.
   Answer: False
8. A deviant member should always be directly confronted about his or her behavior.
   Answer: False
9. Assigning specific tasks to an apathetic member can often increase that member's involvement in the group.
   Answer: True
10. Functional theory assumes that all members can help achieve a group's goal by performing various task and maintenance functions.
    Answer: True

Essay

1. The Functional Theory of group participation identifies task, maintenance, and self-centered group roles. Identify and explain two roles in each category. Provide examples of behavior for each role you identify.
2. Myers-Briggs® personality type theory divides personalities into four major categories with opposite preferences in each category. Identify and explain each of the eight personality types. How can each type contribute to an effective group?
3. The authors of your textbook maintain that overcoming the problem of member apathy is critical to the success of a group. How does apathy affect a group's work? What are some of the causes of apathy in a group? How can a group lessen the effects of apathy?
4. Discuss five responsibilities of participants in a group.
5. The textbook discusses three ways of handling disruptive members. Discuss the three methods and indicate when each is best used.
6. What are hidden agendas and how can they affect a group's work? How should a group deal with the hidden agendas of its members?
7. The authors of your textbook claim that effective group participants must be ready, willing, and able to contribute to a group's goal. Discuss the distinctions between ready, willing, and able. What are the consequences for a group when a member lacks any one of these prerequisites for participation?

8. Hofstede and Hall have identified five dimensions of culture. Identify the five and indicate how they impact participant behavior in a group.
9. Identify the five dimensions of culture that you believe best represent your own orientation. Provide examples of how that has affected your participation within groups.
10. Discuss some of the difficulties of participating in virtual groups. Include in your answer an indication of methods of handling those difficulties.

Chapter 4
Confidence in Groups

Multiple Choice

1. The fear or anxiety associated with either real or anticipated communication with another person or persons is referred to as
   a. self-concept.
   b. feedback.
   Δ c. communication apprehension.
   d. social tension.
   e. confidence.

2. Highly apprehensive group members
   a. are less intelligent than other members.
   b. are less hard-working than other members.
   c. are more intelligent than other members.
   d. are more likely to be seen as leaders.
   Δ e. may still participate and express opinions.

3. What percent of the general population experiences very high levels of communication apprehension?
   a. 10 %
   Δ b. 20 %
   c. 30 %
   d. 40 %
   e. 50 %

4. Which of the following descriptions is likely to be true of highly apprehensive group members?
   a. Apprehensive members talk more in group discussions.
   b. Apprehensive members focus on what they have to say rather than on their internal feelings.
   c. Apprehensive members feel comfortable engaging in conflict within the group.
   Δ d. Apprehensive members are seen as less confident and assertive than other members.
   e. All of the above.

5. The social unease and inhibitions that accompany the getting-acquainted stage in a group is described as
   a. low apprehension.
   b. high apprehension.
   Δ c. primary tension.
   d. secondary tension.
   e. receptivity to feedback.

6. Which of the following behaviors is NOT a symptom of primary tension?
   a. Members avoid interrupting each other.
   Δ b. The group is noisy and physically active.
   c. Members are overly polite.
   d. The group engages in irrelevant small talk.
   e. All of the above.

7. The frustration and personality conflicts experienced by group members as they compete for social acceptance and achievement are sources of
   a. low apprehension.
   b. high apprehension.
   c. primary tension.
   Δ d. secondary tension.
   e. receptivity to feedback.

8. Which of the following items is NOT a symptom of secondary tension?
   a. There is a high level of energy and agitation within the group.
   b. The group is noisy and physically active.
   c. Members speak in loud voices and interrupt each other.
   d. Members tend to lean forward and sit up in their seats.
   Δ e. All of the above.

9. According to your textbook, effective feedback reveals your
   a. readiness, willingness, and ability.
   b. confidence.
   c. apprehension.
   Δ d. feelings, thoughts, and wants.
   e. None of the above.

10. A group member has just suggested an idea. You smile and nod indicating your approval of the suggestion. Your behavior would be described as
   Δ a. feedback.
   b. low apprehension.
   c. high apprehension.
   d. secondary tension.
   e. nonresponsive.

11. According to McCroskey and Richmond, "almost all of the population reports being scared about communicating with a person or group at some point in their lives." What percent of the population is this?
   a. 25 %
   b. 45 %
   c. 65 %
   d. 85 %
   Δ e. 95 %

12. Walther's theory of hyperpersonal communication in virtual groups indicates individuals
    a. ask more personal questions of other group members.
    b. ask less personal questions of other group members.
    c. are less confident in mediated settings than in face-to-face settings.
    Δ d. are more confident in mediated settings than face-to-face meetings.
    e. None of the above.

13. Walther believes individuals may be more confident in mediated group settings because
    a. writing apprehension is nonexistent.
    b. the written message is separate from other personal factors.
    c. members have more time to construct a suitable response.
    d. Both a and b.
    Δ e. Both a and c.

14. Which of the following is NOT a symptom of secondary tension?
    a. Personality conflicts arise.
    b. There is a high level of energy and activity.
    c. Members interrupt one another.
    Δ d. Members avoid expressing strong opinions.
    e. Members speak in louder voices.

15. When expressed appropriately, assertive behavior
    a. can help resolve primary and secondary tension.
    b. can raise confidence levels.
    c. can reduce communication apprehension.
    Δ d. All of the above.
    e. Both b and c.

16. Which of the following is NOT a characteristic of nonassertive group members?
    a. They are reluctant to express opinions.
    b. They fear criticism from others.
    Δ c. They feel a greater sense of power.
    d. They may experience high levels of communication apprehension.
    e. They are rarely satisfied with the group experience.

17. Which of the following is NOT characteristic of aggressive group members?
    a. They act in their own self-interest.
    b. They are critical and combative.
    c. They may become abusive.
    Δ d. They are more highly respected.
    e. They are rarely satisfied with the group experience.

18. Which of the following is NOT a means of providing constructive feedback?
    a. Focusing on the behaviors rather than the person.
    b. Describing the behavior rather than judging it.
    c. Providing observations rather than assumptions.
    d. Choosing an appropriate time and place.
    Δ e. Giving feedback to advancing your own goals.

19. Which of the following is NOT a characteristic of passive-aggressive group members?
    a. They undermine others behind their backs.
    b. They rarely exhibit aggressive behaviors.
    Δ c. They usually follow through with promised contributions.
    d. They have little respect for the rights of others.
    e. They usually behave cooperatively.

20. Which of the following is likely to be true of highly apprehensive group members?
    a. They are viewed as less confident than others.
    b. They are less likely to be leaders.
    c. They are viewed as less responsible than others.
    d. Both a and b.
    Δ e. All of the above.

True/False

1. Communication apprehension occurs only in a public speaking situation.
   Answer: False

2. Providing feedback guarantees that group members will understand your ideas.
   Answer: False

3. Many North Americans fear public speaking more than they fear death.
   Answer: True

4. There is nothing a group can do to help members who suffer from high levels of communication apprehension.
   Answer: False

5. Primary tension and communication apprehension are related.
   Answer: True

6. Being receptive to feedback usually has a negative effect on a member's self-concept.
   Answer: False

7. Members who speak less tend to view the group more negatively.
   Answer: True

8. Group members who speak more are often better liked than those who speak infrequently.
   Answer: True

9. A person's level of communication apprehension is consistent in all situations.
   Answer: False

10. People suffer from communication apprehension because they are less competent than their more confident colleagues.
    Answer: False

Essay

1. Napier and Gershenfeld contend that "in a group, honest feedback can increase accuracy, instill a sense of being understood, and promote closeness and a sense of confidence." Why is this statement accepted as true? Provide examples to support your answer.

2. McCroskey and Richmond claim that communication apprehension is a significant factor in predicting communication behavior in small groups. How does communication apprehension affect group interaction? What are some strategies that high apprehensives can use to help reduce their level of fear? What can low apprehensives do to reduce another member's communication apprehension?

3. What is the difference between primary and secondary tension? Describe the types of behavior typical of a group experiencing each type of tension. What are the consequences for a group that does not successfully move beyond primary and secondary tension?

4. Define and distinguish between the concepts of assertion and aggression. Include in your answer an indication of the impact each has on group communication.

5. You are a member of a group in which you feel confident and comfortable communicating with others. However, another member appears to feel uncomfortable participating in the group's discussions. Assuming this member experiences higher levels of communication apprehension than the other group members, what might you do to help reduce that member's level of apprehension?

6. Walther advances a theory of hyperpersonal communication in virtual groups. Describe the concept and explain what he believes is responsible for its existence.

7. The textbook discusses several methods for building skills in assertion. Identify those methods and discuss the relative complexity of those suggestions.

8. The textbook discusses several strategies for low apprehensive individuals to assist high apprehensive individuals. Identify and discuss those strategies.

9. Discuss the concept of constructive feedback. Include in your answer both an explanation of what it is and how it can be provided.

10. The textbook identifies several strategies for high apprehensives to cope with communication apprehension. Identify and discuss those strategies.

Chapter 5
Verbal and Nonverbal Communication in Groups

Multiple Choice

1. At a regular study group meeting, one member asks that everyone be able to "summarize the most important information in each chapter." At the next meeting, another member distributes an outline of the textbook's important concepts but wonders why no one else in the group has made the same effort. This misunderstanding is an example of
   a. failure to *follow* the rules of language.
   b. denotation.
   c. failure to interpret nonverbal behavior.
   Δ d. bypassing.
   e. concrete words.

2. Defining a computer as "a programmable electronic device that stores, retrieves, and processes data" represents what type of meaning?
   a. Bypassing
   Δ b. Denotation
   c. Connotation
   d. Abstract
   e. All of the above.

3. If the word "computer" evokes a negative image of a complicated machine that easily frustrates you, what type of meaning is influencing your response to the word?
   a. Bypassing
   b. Denotation
   Δ c. Connotation
   d. Concrete
   e. Jargon

4. Which of the following is an example of an abstract word?
   a. Meeting
   b. Table
   c. Computer
   d. Dictionary
   Δ e. Fairness

5. Which of the following would be considered the most concrete description of a member's behavior?
   a. Disruptive
   b. Rude during a discussion
   c. Insensitive to others
   Δ d. Uses profanity
   e. All of the above.

6. The specialized or technical language of a profession is referred to as
   a. denotative.
   b. dialects.
   c. concrete.
   d. abstract.
   Δ e. jargon.

7. The study of body movement and physical expression is referred to as
   Δ a. kinesics.
   b. word stress.
   c. proxemics.
   d. yerritoriality.
   e. polychronic.

8. According to Judee Burgoon, when engaging in cooperative activities, group members usually prefer
   Δ a. side-by-side seats.
   b. seats across from each other.
   c. seats in rows.
   d. a seat at the head of the table.
   e. All of the above.

9. The use of emoticons in virtual groups
   a. are generally effective substitutes for nonverbal communication.
   Δ b. are generally ineffective substitutes for nonverbal communication.
   c. should always be avoided.
   d. have a great impact on communicative meaning.
   e. should only be used when they are easily recognized.

10. Which distance would most people typically use for a conversation with a friend or close acquaintance?
    a. Intimate distance
    Δ b. Personal distance
    c. Social distance
    d. Private distance
    e. Public distance

11. Group members who prefer to carefully schedule all activities, manage their time carefully, and work on one task at a time are using a(n) __________ approach to time.
    a. multichronic
    b. polychronic
    Δ c. monochronic
    d. ambichronic
    e. microchronic

12. The statement "That's a stupid way to approach the problem." is an example of which type of response?
    a. Descriptive
    Δ b. Evaluative
    c. Problem-oriented
    d. Strategic
    e. Empathetic

13. Jack Gibb has described six pairs of communication behaviors that influence whether a group's climate is defensive or supportive. Which of the following communication behaviors is the opposite of evaluation?
    a. Control
    b. Problem orientation
    c. Strategy
    d. Superiority
    Δ e. Description

14. The use of plural pronouns in the statement "Let's keep working on this until we're ready for lunch." is an indicator of which team talk dimension?
    Δ a. Identification
    b. Interdependence
    c. Power differentiation
    d. Social distance
    e. Negotiation process

15. Deborah Tannen compares the differences between male and female communication to that of different cultures. She maintains that, in many situations, men and women use language differently. Men are more likely to
    a. use communication to maintain relationships and cooperate with others.
    Δ b. leave out details in order to get directly to the point.
    c. include qualifiers and tag questions in their sentences.
    d. provide more supporting or explanatory details before getting to the point.
    e. speak tentatively.

16. In reviewing the research on dialects, Dodd has drawn several conclusions. Which statement is NOT one of Dodd's conclusions?
    a. People judge others by their speech.
    b. Upward mobility and social aspirations influence whether people change their speech to the accepted norms.
    Δ c. It would be unethical to speak differently at home than you would speak at work.
    d. General American speech is most accepted by the majority of the American culture.
    e. People should be aware of these prejudices and attempt to look beyond the surface.

17. _______________ is the means we use to achieve group goals, the stimulus we use to build relationships, and the evidence we use to assess group work.
   a. Connotation
   b. Bypassing
   c. Climate
Δ d. Team talk
   e. Provisionalism

18. Which of the following is NOT a strategy for improving a group's team talk?
Δ a. Expressing individual needs.
   b. Use of the pronouns "we," "us," and "our".
   c. Listen to dissenters.
   d. Speak in a specific and active voice.
   e. Ask more "what if" questions.

19. The variations in vocabulary, pronunciation, syntax, and style that distinguish speakers from different ethnic groups and geographic areas are referred to as
   a. denotative
Δ b. dialects
   c. codeswitching
   d. abstract
   e. jargon

20. Posture, touch, and gestures are examples of
   a. territoriality.
   b. intimate distance.
   c. denotation.
   d. polychronics.
Δ e. kinesics.

True/False

1. Members' tone of voice, eye contact, and physical proximity can tell you as much or more about their thoughts and feelings than the words they speak.
   Answer: True

2. The ability to follow the accepted rules of our language has very little influence on others' perceptions of our intelligence and social status.
   Answer: False

3. Denotation, rather than connotation, is more likely to influence how we respond to words.
   Answer: False

4. Abstract words refer to an idea or concept that cannot be observed or touched.
   Answer: True

5. Male speech is generally characterized as more direct and forceful than female speech.
   Answer: True

6. Bypassing is the means we use to achieve group goals, the stimulus we use to build group relationships, and the evidence we use to assess group work.
   Answer: False

7. The face is capable of expressing more varied emotion than any other part of the body.
   Answer: True

8. In denotative language, a word always has only one meaning.
   Answer: False

9. Superordinate terms are those with the highest level of concreteness.
   Answer: False

10. The use of jargon is always counterproductive in communication.
    Answer: False

Essay

1. When comparing the differences between male and female communication, Deborah Tannen writes that "they speak different genderlects." What does Tannen mean by this statement? What are the differences between the ways in which males and females use language? How can these two approaches affect group interaction?

2. You are responsible for arranging a room for a meeting of 12 people. In the room are 4 tables 6 feet in length and 12 chairs. Draw an arrangement that would discourage group interaction among group members. Why does this arrangement discourage interaction? Draw an arrangement that would promote the maximum amount of group interaction. Why does this arrangement encourage interaction?

3. Jack Gibb has described six pairs of communication behaviors that influence whether a group's climate is defensive or supportive. Identify and explain all six pairs of behaviors. How does each type of behavior affect a group's climate?

4. What is team talk? Identify and describe each of Donnellon's six dimensions of team talk. Provide an example of each. How can understanding team talk improve group communication?

5. Identify and explain each of Hall's zones of interaction. Which zones of interaction are groups more likely to use?

6. What is sexist language? What effect can the use of sexist language have on a group? What can members do to avoid sexist language?

7. Cook identifies three levels of linguistic abstraction. Explain the different levels and provide a specific example to illustrate your point.

8. Discuss the role that jargon plays in the communicative process. Include in your answer an indication of both the advantages and disadvantages of its usage.

9. Discuss the concept of code-switching. Include in your answer an indication both of what it is and examples of when it might be used.

10. Discuss the impact of culture on nonverbal communication. Include in your answer a discussion of specific differences in members of different cultural groups.

Chapter 6
Listening in Groups

Multiple Choice

1. The ability to understand, analyze, respect, and respond to the meaning of another person's spoken and nonverbal messages defines
   a. feedback.
   Δ b. listening.
   c. self-centered listening.
   d. the golden listening rule.
   e. All of the above.

2. Studies have found that listening occupies _______________ of a college student's communicating time.
   a. less than 10 %
   b. less than 30 %
   Δ c. more than 50 %
   d. more than 70 %
   e. about 95 %

3. According to Ralph Nichols, without listening training most people listen at ______ efficiency.
   a. 15 %
   Δ b. 25 %
   c. 35 %
   d. 45 %
   e. 55 %

4. Your group has invited an expert to speak about the American Disabilities Act and its implications for an event the group is planning. Your primary goal during the presentation is to make sure you understand what the speaker has to say about the law. What type of listening should be your focus?
   a. Analytical listening
   b. Empathic listening
   Δ c. Comprehensive listening
   d. Appreciative listening
   e. Self-centered listening

5. The group has suggested that a meeting be scheduled for Saturday morning. Nicole seems upset. You want to understand how she feels about the proposed meeting. When she explains her concerns, you should focus your efforts on
   a. analytical listening.
   Δ b. empathic listening.
   c. comprehensive listening.
   d. appreciative listening.
   e. self-centered listening.

6. Two committee members have made different recommendations for the date of the company's annual picnic. Which type of listening will help you decide which suggestion to support?
Δ a. Analytical listening
b. Empathic listening
c. Comprehensive listening
d. Appreciative listening
e. Self-centered listening

7. What type of listening enables you to acknowledge a member's effective use of language, ability to use humor, and skillful presentation of arguments?
a. Critical listening
b. Empathic listening
c. Comprehensive listening
Δ d. Appreciative listening
e. Self-centered listening

8. A good listener will use his or her extra thought speed to
Δ a. summarize main ideas.
b. take word-for-word notes.
c. plan how to confront the speaker.
d. engage in side conversations.
e. daydream.

9. Which of the following is NOT true of self-centered listeners?
a. They put their own needs ahead of the group's needs.
b. They may be excellent listeners.
Δ c. They are always poor listeners.
d. They may perform a blocking role in communication.
e. They may serve as special interest pleaders.

10. _______________ is the ability to restate what people say in a way that indicates you have understood what they mean.
a. Self-listening
b. Taking notes
c. Appreciative listening
Δ d. Paraphrasing
e. Maintenance listening

11. Which of the following statements represents the best paraphrase of "if we don't get this job done on time, the boss will be furious"?
a. Who cares? We're doing the right thing. Right?
b. Don't worry. As long as we stick together we'll be okay.
Δ c. You seem very concerned about the boss's reaction to completing this project on schedule. Is that your worry?
d. You don't have any confidence in our group's ability—or do you?
e. How do you know the boss will be furious?

12. What type of listening enables you to accurately understand the meaning of group members' spoken and nonverbal messages?
Δ a. Comprehensive listening
b. Empathic listening
c. Analytical listening
d. Appreciative listening
e. Self-centered listening

13. What type of listening enables you to form appropriate opinions about the content of a messsage?
a. Comprehensive listening
b. Empathic listening
Δ c. Analytical listening
d. Appreciative listening
e. Self-centered listening

14. What type of listening enables you to understand and identify a person's feelings or motives?
a. Comprehensive listening
Δ b. Empathic listening
c. Analytical listening
d. Appreciative listening
e. Self-centered listening

15. Empathic listening can be improved by
a. being conscious of your feedback.
b. focusing on the speaker, not yourself.
c. avoiding any nonverbal feedback.
Δ d. Both a and b.
e. All of the above.

16. Analytical listening can be improved by
a. recognizing persuasive strategies.
b. evaluating persuasive strategies.
c. maintaining a strong belief in your own position.
Δ d. Both a and b.
e. All of the above.

17. Appreciative listening can be improved by
a. setting aside time for appreciative listening.
b. preparing to listen appreciatively.
c. welcoming opportunities to hear something challenging.
d. Both a and b.
Δ e. All of the above.

18. Task-oriented members tend to be particularly effective at
  Δ a. comprehensive and analytical listening.
  b. comprehensive and empathic listening.
  c. comprehensive and appreciative listening.
  d. analytical and empathic listening.
  e. analytical and appreciative listening.

19. Maintenance-oriented members tend to be particularly effective at
  a. empathic and comprehensive listening.
  b. empathic and analytical listening.
  Δ c. empathic and appreciative listening.
  d. comprehensive and analytical listening.
  e. comprehensive and appreciative listening.

20. Which of the following is NOT a characteristic of paraphrasing?
  a. It is the ability to restate what a person has said.
  b. It is a form of feedback.
  Δ c. It is the ability to repeat what a person has said.
  d. It usually includes a request for confirmation.
  e. It can be used for many purposes.

True/False

1. Listening and hearing are the same thing.
Answer: False

2. Listening is our number one communication activity.
Answer: True

3. Members who assume self-centered roles may be excellent listeners or poor listeners.
Answer: True

4. Most people can speak much faster than they can think.
Answer: False

5. Differences in listening skills, gender, personality types, and cultural backgrounds can affect a group's ability to listen.
Answer: True

6. The social pressure to listen is greater in groups than it is in a conversation with just one person.
Answer: False

7. Members who excel in task and maintenance roles are often skilled listeners.
Answer: True

8. Women are more likely to listen to the content of what is said, while men tend to focus on the relationships among speakers.
Answer: False

9. Personnel managers have identified effective listening as the most important communication skill.
Answer: True

10. Evaluating evidence while it is being presented interferes with good listening skills.
Answer: False

Essay

1. According to the textbook, there are four types of listening that are important to small group communication. Identify and explain each of the four types of listening. Provide an example of each type of listening within a group context.
2. The authors of your textbook claim that members who assume task and maintenance roles are often good listeners. What types of listening do members in task roles often use? What types of listening do members in maintenance roles often use? How do self-centered roles affect listening?
3. Several studies have concluded that while we spend a significant amount of our communication time listening, many of us are not very effective listeners. Identify and explain three strategies that a group member could follow to improve his or her listening.
4. Why is listening more difficult in groups than in almost any other communication situation? Justify and support your answer with examples.
5. Identify and explain the "golden listening rule." What must a listener do in order to follow the rule? How does the rule result in more effective listening?
6. As important as it is to listen to other members of your group, it is just as important to listen to yourself. Your textbook suggests seven questions to ask yourself in order to better monitor your internal thought process. Identify and explain the seven questions.
7. Wolvin and Coakley have identified six positive listening attitudes and their negative counterparts. Identify and explain the six pairs.
8. Listening has been described as more difficult in groups than in any other communication situation. Indicate whether you agree or disagree with that conclusion and justify your position.
9. Discuss the concept of self-centered listening. Include in your answer both an explanation of what it is and how it impacts the group process.
10. Discuss the concept of listening in virtual groups. Include in your answer an indication of both the benefits and weaknesses of listening in such groups.

Chapter 7
Conflict and Cohesion in Groups

Multiple Choice

1. The members of a civic association's committee on community safety disagree on whether to install more expensive street lighting throughout the development. What type of conflict is the group experiencing?
   a. Affective
   b. Collaborative
Δ c. Substantive
   d. Competitive
   e. Procedural

2. The members of a committee to address safety issues in a community disagree over whether to first survey the residents or to begin by consulting local law enforcement for safety suggestions. What type of conflict is the group experiencing?
   a. Affective
   b. Collaborative
   c. Substantive
   d. Competitive
Δ e. Procedural

3. Joe gets angry with Delores during a committee meeting because she interrupts his remarks and suggests that his ideas are a waste of time. What type of conflict is occurring in this situation?
Δ a. Affective
   b. Collaborative
   c. Substantive
   d. Competitive
   e. Procedural

4. Which of the following statements characterizes constructive conflict?
Δ a. Members focus on the issues.
   b. Members' contributions are devalued.
   c. Members protect and defend their own ideas.
   d. Members avoid conflict.
   e. Members resist change and try to maintain traditional procedures.

5. Tran tries to change the subject when group members argue. She also refuses to comment on controversial issues. What conflict style does Tran use?
   a. Accommodation
   b. Collaboration
   c. Competition
Δ d. Avoidance
   e. Compromise

6. When a member is more concerned with his or her own goals rather than meeting the needs of the group, which conflict style is the member using?
   a. Accommodation
   b. Collaboration
   Δ c. Competition
   d. Avoidance
   e. Compromise

7. Some club members want to increase membership dues by $7.00. Other club members want to increase them by $3.00. They have reached an impasse on the issue so they decide to split the difference and raise the dues by $5.00. What type of conflict style did the group use?
   a. Accommodation
   b. Collaboration
   c. Competition
   d. Avoidance
   Δ e. Compromise

8. Family members disagree about where to go for a vacation this year. Some members want a location where there will be a lot to do. Other members just want to relax. They discuss many possible sites before deciding on a cruise. They agree that a cruise offers opportunities for both relaxation and recreation. Which approach to conflict did this family use?
   a. Accommodation
   Δ b. Collaboration
   c. Competition
   d. Avoidance
   e. Compromise

9. Which of the following methods is NOT a suggested way of dealing with anger in a group?
   a. Use "I" statements
   b. Apply the golden listening rule
   Δ c. Make accusations
   d. Describe your anger and its source
   e. Allow other group members to express their anger

10. Which method of conflict resolution employs the services of an impartial third party for the purpose of guiding, coaching, and encouraging the disputants toward agreement?
   a. Arbitration
   Δ b. Mediation
   c. Negotiation
   d. The 4Rs method
   e. The A-E-I-O-U model

11. Which of the following statements is characteristic of a cohesive group?
    a. Members interact with each other less.
    b. Members make a lot of negative statements about the group.
    Δ c. The group exerts greater influence over members to conform to group expectations.
    d. The group lacks creativity.
    e. None of the above.

12. Which symptom of groupthink is expressed when a group member confronts another by saying "Why aren't you in favor of this? You're the only one who's against it. Give it up!"?
    a. Rationalization
    b. Self-censorship
    c. Mindguarding
    Δ d. Pressure on dissent
    e. Illusion of invulnerability

13. Which of the following is NOT a principle of groups committed to constructive conflict?
    a. Members work to achieve a mutually satisfying resolution of a conflict.
    b. Disagreement is not punished.
    Δ c. Lower status members will avoid disagreeing with higher status members.
    d. There is an agreed-upon approach for conflict resolution.
    e. Members may disagree and still respect one another.

14. Which of the following are characteristics of a cohesive group?
    a. High levels of interaction.
    b. The use of creative approaches to achieving goals.
    c. A desire to challenge group expectations.
    Δ d. Both a and b.
    e. All of the above.

15. Which of the following is NOT a characteristic of groupthink?
    a. Overconfidence
    b. Discounting of warnings
    c. Stereotype of outsiders
    d. Mindguarding
    Δ e. None of the above.

16. When a member attempts to change the topic, which conflict style is a member using?
    a. Accommodation
    Δ b. Avoidance
    c. Collaboration
    d. Competition
    e. Compromise

17. When a member gives in to others at the expense of his or her own goals, what conflict style is the member using?
    a. Collaboration
    b. Compromise
    c. Avoidance
Δ d. Accommodation
    e. Competition

18. When a member searches for new solutions that will achieve both the individual goals of group members and the group goals, what conflict style is the member using?
    a. Competition
    b. Avoidance
Δ c. Collaboration
    d. Accommodation
    e. Compromise

19. When a member concedes some goals in order to achieve others, what conflict style is the member using?
Δ a. Compromise
    b. Collaboration
    c. Avoidance
    d. Accommodation
    e. Competition

20. Which of the following is NOT part of the 4R method of Conflict Management?
    a. Reasons
    b. Reactions
    c. Results
Δ d. Reinterpretation
    e. Resolution

True/False

1. Preset methods for conflict resolution are counterproductive.
   Answer: False

2. All conflict in groups is destructive and should be avoided if at all possible.
   Answer: False

3. The collaborative approach to conflict works best in all situations.
   Answer: False

4. A mediator does not take sides in a dispute.
   Answer: True

5. Highly cohesive groups are at greater risk of succumbing to groupthink.
   Answer: True

6. In general, men tend to approach conflict more collaboratively.
   Answer: False

7. Email messages can increase the likelihood of conflict in a virtual group.
   Answer: True

8. Negotiation and mediation are two terms for the same process.
   Answer: False

9. Groupthink is more likely to occur in highly cohesive groups.
   Answer: True

10. Avoidance is always useful as a conflict style.
    Answer: False

Essay

1. Thomas and Kilmann have described five conflict styles. Identify and explain each style. Under what circumstances would each style be appropriate? Which style fulfills everyone's interests without requiring significant sacrifices from individual members?

2. Wisinski's A-E-I-O-U Model of conflict resolution is a way to communicate concerns and suggest alternative actions. Using an example of a group conflict, identify and explain each step of the model.

3. The 4Rs method can be used to analyze group conflict. What does each of the 4Rs stand for? What questions does each R suggest for analyzing the nature and management of conflict in groups?

4. What is groupthink? What are the symptoms of groupthink? How does this phenomenon affect group decision making? What are some ways to prevent or deal with groupthink?

5. What is the difference between constructive and destructive conflict in a group? What effect does destructive conflict have on a group? How does constructive conflict affect a group?

6. The textbook identifies three types of conflict. Identify and explain the three types. Use examples to illustrate your points.

7. Discuss the basic principles that should guide a group committed to constructive conflict. Include examples in your discussion.

8. Discuss the factors that contribute to increased conflict in virtual groups. Include examples in your discussion.

9. Negotiation in a group may become deadlocked. Discuss several of the strategies that can be used to help break a deadlock.

10. Assume you have been selected as a mediator in a conflict among members of your youth group. Describe the steps you would follow in the mediated session.

Chapter 8
Leadership in Groups

Multiple Choice

1. At the end of every month, a sales manager offers a cash bonus to the most successful salesperson. What type of power is this leader using?
   a. Referent power
   b. Coercive power
   Δ c. Reward power
   d. Legitimate power
   e. Expert power

2. A supervisor threatens to dismiss any member of the sales team who does not meet the sales quota by the end of the quarter. What type of power is this leader using?
   a. Referent power
   Δ b. Coercive power
   c. Reward power
   d. Legitimate power
   e. Expert power

3. You have been promoted to a management position within your place of business. You expect employees to fulfill your requests because you are the boss. What type of power is this?
   a. Referent power
   b. Coercive power
   c. Reward power
   Δ d. Legitimate power
   e. Expert power

4. Which category of power is operating when a group member nominates someone as a leader by saying, "I recommend that Romero be appointed chair of the building committee given his experience as a successful contractor."?
   a. Referent power
   b. Coercive power
   c. Reward power
   d. Legitimate power
   Δ e. Expert power

5. Your group has chosen Madeleine as its leader because she has demonstrated strong organizational and problem-solving skills as well as a talent for motivating members and resolving conflict. What type of power does Madeleine have?
   Δ a. Referent power
   b. Coercive power
   c. Reward power
   d. Legitimate power
   e. Expert power

6. Which of the following behaviors is NOT a recommended strategy for becoming a group leader?
   a. Talking early.
   b. Talking often.
   c. Knowing more about important topics.
   Δ d. Not offering your own opinion.
   e. Volunteering for meaningful roles.

7. Vu tries to maintain strict control over the Spring Festival planning committee. He insists on controlling the direction and outcome of the committee's discussion. Which leadership style is Vu using?
   a. Democratic
   Δ b. Autocratic
   c. Situational
   d. Laissez-faire
   e. Functional

8. As chairperson of the PTA's election committee, Vicky believes in practicing social equality. She shares decision making with the group. Which leadership style is Vicky using?
   Δ a. Democratic
   b. Autocratic
   c. Situational
   d. Laissez-faire
   e. Functional

9. Which of the following is NOT a strategy for becoming a leader?
   a. Talking early and often.
   b. Sharing information.
   c. Listening to others.
   d. Welcoming disagreement.
   Δ e. All of the above.

10. Even though Wayne is chairperson of the finance committee, he does little or nothing to help the group. He tends to let the group take charge of all decisions and actions. Which leadership style is Wayne using?
   a. Democratic
   b. Autocratic
   c. Situational
   Δ d. Laissez-faire
   e. Functional

11. Which theory of leadership explains how leaders can become more effective once they have carefully analyzed themselves, their group, and the circumstances in which they must lead?
    a. Trait theory
    b. Style theory
Δ   c. Situational theory
    d. Functional theory
    e. Emergence theory

12. If "task-motivated" describes your leadership style, Fiedler's Contingency Model of Leadership Effectiveness predicts that you will be least successful when
    a. the group's task is highly structured.
    b. there are poor leader-member relationships.
    c. you have a great deal of reward, coercive, and legitimate power.
    d. you have no power.
Δ   e. you have a moderate degree of power and task structure.

13. Emergent leaders tend to achieve power
    a. gradually.
    b. by contributing to the achievement of group goals.
    c. as a result of hidden agendas.
Δ   d. Both a and b.
    e. Both b and c.

14. Autocratic leaders
    a. are always counterproductive.
    b. make many of the group's decisions.
    c. expect followers to obey orders.
    d. Both a and b.
Δ   e. Both b and c.

15. Laissez-faire leaders
    a. let the group take charge of decisions and actions.
    b. work well in mature and highly productive groups.
    c. may generate a climate of open communication.
    d. Both a and b.
Δ   e. All of the above.

16. The Functional Theory of Leadership
    a. assumes one person is an obvious leader in a group.
Δ   b. does not assume leadership is the responsibility of one person.
    c. assumes that people are born as leaders.
    d. places a high priority on the leader's personality.
    e. concludes that leadership is unnecessary.

17. The characteristic that most distinguishes transformational leadership is
    a. intelligence.
    b. passion.
    c. creativity.
Δ   d. vision.
    e. charisma.

18. Modeling Leadership Behaviors includes
    a. publicly championing your group and its goals.
    b. behaving consistently and assertively.
    c. maintaining control at all times.
Δ   d. Both a and b.
    e. Both b and c.

19. Which of the following is NOT a characteristic of effective decision making by a leader?
    a. The ability to make timely decisions.
    b. The ability to provide a rationale for decisions.
Δ   c. The ability to make the most popular decisions.
    d. The willingness to solicit feedback.
    e. The ability to clearly communicate the decision to the group.

20. Members from uncertainty avoidance cultures want
Δ   a. more structure and instructions from a leader.
    b. less structure and instructions from a leader.
    c. more nurturing from a leader.
    d. less nurturing from a leader.
    e. a closer relationship with a leader.

True/False

1. Emergent leaders are deliberately and purposely selected by a group or an outside authority.
   Answer: False

2. Trait theory suggests that leaders are born, not made.
   Answer: True

3. The democratic leadership style is always best.
   Answer: False

4. Task-motivated leaders gain satisfaction from completing a task even if the cost is bad feelings between the leader and group members.
   Answer: True

5. The functional theory of leadership assumes that leadership is the sole responsibility of one person-the leader.
   Answer: False

6. A group can have more than one leader.
   Answer: True

7. Transformational leaders tend to be reluctant to take risks.
   Answer: False

8. Multiple leaders are the exception rather than the rule in virtual groups.
   Answer: False

9. Women are less likely than men to be pre-selected as leaders.
   Answer: True

10. Minority leaders do not differ from dominant culture leaders in behavior, performance, or member satisfaction.
   Answer: True

Essay

1. French and Raven have divided power into five categories. Identify and explain each type of power and its implications for leadership. Provide an example of each type of power.

2. The authors of your textbook recommend several strategies for becoming a leader. Explain three of these strategies. Why does each strategy increase the likelihood that a member will become the leader of his or her group?

3. The styles theory of leadership describes three types of leaders. Identify and explain each style. What are the strengths and weaknesses of each style?

4. According to Fiedler's Contingency Model of Leadership Effectiveness there are ideal matches between leadership style and group situations. Describe the ideal match for a task-motivated leader and a relationship-motivated leader.

5. A leader who has been chosen from the group to lead his or her peers faces unique leadership challenges. Why is this often a difficult situation? What might a new leader in such a situation do to successfully deal with these difficulties?

6. Discuss the concept of transformational leadership. Include in your answer both a definition of the concept and several characteristics of transformational leaders. Identify one person you believe to be a transformational leader.

7. Identify and discuss the four functions found in the 4M Model of Leadership Effectiveness.

8. Discuss the difficulties women have in achieving leadership positions. Indicate whether you believe such difficulties are increasing, decreasing or remaining the same and explain your reasoning.

9. Discuss the implications that cultural diversity has for leadership, both in terms of attainment and conduct.

10. Perceptions of George W. Bush's leadership skills changed drastically after 9/11/02. Using concepts from the text, explain what you believe to be responsible for the changing perceptions.

Chapter 9
Decision Making and Problem Solving in Groups

Multiple Choice

1. Which of the following statements is NOT true about decision making in groups?
   Δ a. Groups usually take less time to make a decision than an individual working alone.
   b. A group generates more ideas than an individual working alone.
   c. Groups generally produce better decisions than individuals.
   d. All of the above.
   e. None of the above.

2. A company's recycling task force is composed of fifteen members. If the task force makes decisions based on a consensus, how many members must be in favor of the group decision?
   a. 5
   b. 7
   c. 8
   d. 10
   Δ e. 15

3. Which of the following is NOT considered a guideline for brainstorming?
   a. Evaluate ideas only at the end.
   b. Post the ideas for all to see.
   c. Wait awhile before starting the brainstorming.
   Δ d. Avoid combining ideas.
   e. Do not praise another member's ideas.

4. You should consider using DOT when the group
   a. has generated a significant number of competing ideas.
   b. is limited in time.
   c. wants to ensure equal opportunity for input
   Δ d. All of the above.
   e. Both b and c.

5. A company's recycling task force gathered information on various recycling programs and met several times to choose which program would best suit the needs of the company. The group's recommendation was presented to the company's vice president of operations who ultimately chose a program other than the one recommended by the task force. Which method of decision making was used in this situation?
   Δ a. Authority rule
   b. Consensus
   c. Majority vote
   d. Minority rule
   e. Two-thirds vote

6. “How many employees hire a day care provider to watch their children during the workday?” This group discussion question represents a question of
   a. policy.
   b. procedure.
Δ c. fact.
   d. conjecture.
   e. value.

7. “Is it appropriate for parents to bring their children to work?” This group discussion question represents a question of
   a. policy.
   b. procedure.
   c. fact.
   d. conjecture.
Δ e. value.

8. “How can the company assist employees with their child care needs?” This group discussion question represents a question of
Δ a. policy.
   b. procedure.
   c. fact.
   d. conjecture.
   e. value.

9. Your group began by making sure everyone understood the assignment before moving on to identify the problem. The group then gathered and analyzed all the facts. Solution criteria were established before suggesting solutions. Next, the group evaluated and selected a solution. Finally, ways to implement the chosen solution were discussed. Which problem-solving method did the group use?
Δ a. The Standard Agenda
   b. The Functional Approach
   c. Nominal Group Technique
   d. PERT
   e. Consensus seeking

10. Which approach to problem solving emphasizes specific communication behaviors rather than the particular sequence of problem-solving steps?
   a. The Standard Agenda
Δ b. The Functional Approach
   c. Nominal Group Technique
   d. Brainstorming
   e. Consensus seeking

11. Your group needs to come up with a discussion topic for a class assignment. The group works together suggesting as many topics as they can. Members are careful never to criticize the suggestions of other members. Which decision-making method is the group using?
    a. The Functional Approach
    b. PERT
    Δ c. Brainstorming
    d. Consensus seeking
    e. Nominal Group Technique

12. Which decision-making tool requires a group to decide how, when, and under what conditions and authority a plan should be implemented?
    a. The Functional Approach
    Δ b. PERT
    c. Brainstorming
    d. Consensus seeking
    e. Nominal Group Technique

13. _______________ was developed by Delbecq and Van de Ven as a way of maximizing participation in problem-solving and program-planning groups while minimizing some of the interpersonal problems associated with group interaction.
    a. The Standard Agenda
    b. Brainstorming
    c. PERT
    Δ d. Nominal Group Technique
    e. Ideal-Solution Format

14. The ideal-solution format is a problem-solving technique designed to
    Δ a. give group members a chance to hear and understand the opinions and needs of others.
    b. plan and coordinate the many steps needed to carry out a solution or agreed-upon action.
    c. allow ideas to be generated by individuals working alone rather than emerging from group interaction.
    d. generate as many ideas as possible in a short period of time.
    e. emphasize specific communication behaviors rather than the sequence of problem-solving steps.

15. "Who will be the next student government president?" This discussion question represents a question of
    a. policy.
    b. procedure.
    c. fact.
    Δ d. conjecture.
    e. value.

16. _______________ are the stages of the creative thinking process.
    a. Inertia; instruction; imitation; innovation
    b. Forming; storming; norming; performing
    c. Reasons; reactions; results; resolution
    d. Identify; isolate; invite; incite
Δ e. Investigation; imagination; incubation; insight

17. A Congressional debate on a bill to increase penalties for fraud committed by business CEOs is a question of
    a. fact.
    b. value.
Δ c. policy.
    d. procedure.
    e. conjecture.

18. Which of the following is NOT a part of the Standard Agenda format?
    a. Task clarification
Δ b. Establishment of procedure
    c. Problem identification
    d. Fact finding
    e. Solution suggestions

19. There are twelve members in your group. How many members must be in favor of a proposal when deciding by authority rule?
Δ a. 1
    b. 6
    c. 7
    d. 10
    e. 12

20. Getting bogged down in analyzing the problem too much is referred to as
    a. groupthink.
    b. conjecture.
    c. consensus.
Δ d. analysis paralysis.
    e. fact finding.

True/False

1. Decision making results in a position, judgement, or action.
   Answer: True
2. Voting is always the best way to make group decisions.
   Answer: False
3. Establishing clear group procedures can provide a group with a sense of control.
   Answer: True
4. It is important that each step of The Functional Approach to problem solving be completed in order.
   Answer: False
5. Groups should ignore the fact that members may have preexisting preferences about what a group should do.
   Answer: False
6. Effective groups produce more ideas than individuals working alone.
   Answer: True
7. Research has identified The Standard Agenda approach as the most effective problem-solving model.
   Answer: False
8. While brainstorming, avoid writing anything down.
   Answer: False
9. DOT is a brainstorming technique intended primarily to generate more ideas.
   Answer: False
10. In virtual groups, all types of technology are not equally suited to all types of group interaction.
    Answer: False

Essay

1. Marshall Scott Poole has called procedures "the heart of group work." What did Poole mean by this statement? Why are procedures important? How does a group benefit from using clear procedures?
2. What are the basic steps in The Standard Agenda? Explain each step and describe what a group should do to accomplish each step. What are the potential consequences of ignoring any one of the steps in The Standard Agenda?
3. The authors of your textbook suggest that politics, preexisting preferences, and power can negatively affect the group process. What are the effects of each of these factors on group decision making? What can a group do to minimize the influence of each of these factors?
4. Discuss the role of creativity in problem solving. What are the stages of the creative process? What are some methods for enhancing group creativity?

5. What is PERT and how is it used in decision making? Using the example of planning an awards banquet, identify and explain each step of the process.
6. LaFasto and Larson suggest that the Single Question Format is an effective method of problem solving. Discuss the five steps in the format and indicate why each step is important.
7. The textbook suggests six guidelines for engaging in brainstorming. Identify and explain the six guidelines.
8. DOT is a decision- making tool. Explain the purpose of the technique and discuss its major steps.
9. Discuss the Functional Theory Approach to problem solving. Include in your answer an explanation of the major conditions that are necessary and provide a specific example of its use.
10. Discuss the Nominal Group Technique of group decision making. Include in your answer an indication of the different phases and indicate when it may best be used.

Chapter 10
Argumentation in Groups

Multiple Choice

1. Which of the following statements is true about constructive argumentation in groups?
   a. It promotes misunderstandings.
Δ b. It promotes critical thinking.
   c. It prevents persuasion.
   d. It promotes groupthink.
   e. It harms group decision making.

2. Which of the following statements best describes a highly argumentative group member?
   a. The member is nonconfrontational.
   b. The member has less influence in group decision making.
Δ c. The member is less likely to be persuaded by others.
   d. The member is less likely to be chosen as the group leader.
   e. All of the above.

3. Which component of the Toulmin Model of argument explains why the data supports the claim?
   a. Qualifier
   b. Data
Δ c. Warrant
   d. Backing
   e. Reservation

4. Which component of the Toulmin Model of argument is represented in Part II of the following argument?
   I. Joan would be a good group leader.
   II. Good leaders have effective communication skills.
   III Joan took a communication course last year.
   a. Claim
   b. Data
Δ c. Warrant
   d. Backing
   e. Reservation

5. Which component of the Toulmin Model of argument is represented in Part I of the following argument?
   I. Joan would be a good group leader.
   II. Good leaders have effective communication skills.
   III. Joan took a communication course last year.
Δ a. Claim
   b. Data
   c. Warrant
   d. Backing
   e. Reservation

6. Which component of the Toulmin Model of argument is represented in Part III of the following argument?
   I. Joan would be a good group leader.
   II. Good leaders have effective communication skills.
   III. Joan took a communication course last year.
   a. Claim
Δ b. Data
   c. Warrant
   d. Backing
   e. Reservation

7. Words in a claim such as "likely," "possibly," or "probably" usually indicate which component of the Toulmin Model of argument?
   a. Reservation
   b. Data
   c. Warrant
   d. Backing
Δ e. Qualifier

8. The act of proving an argument either erroneous or false, or both, is defined as
   a. argumentation.
Δ b. refutation.
   c. argumentativeness.
   d. reasoning.
   e. cooperative argumentation.

9. "The community should enact a curfew for all juveniles." This statement is an example of a claim of
   a. fact.
   b. procedure.
Δ c. policy.
   d. value.
   e. fiction.

10. Some group members have suggested that the company have a picnic instead of the more formal annual dinner. John disagrees with the others because the company has held a formal dinner every year for over ten years. Which fallacy of argument could be attributed to John's comment?
    a. Ad *hominem*
    b. Appeal to authority
    c. Appeal to popularity
    Δ d. Appeal to tradition
    e. Faulty cause

11. When a member insults or attacks the character of another group member, which ethical responsibility has been violated?
    a. The research responsibility.
    b. The common good responsibility.
    c. The reasoning responsibility.
    Δ d. The social code responsibility.
    e. None of the above.

12. Which of the following is NOT true of highly argumentative individuals?
    a. They show genuine interest in a discussion.
    b. They focus on issues rather than personalities.
    Δ c. They actively promote hostility in the group.
    d. They are viewed as high in credibility.
    e. They are often chosen as group leaders.

13. "Our group is the best in the class." This statement is an example of a claim of
    a. Fact
    b. Procedure
    c. Policy
    Δ d. Value
    e. Fiction

14. Which component of the Toulmin Model constitutes the evidence used to support the claim?
    Δ a. Data
    b. Warrant
    c. Qualifier
    d. Reservation
    e. Backing

15. Which component of the Toulmin Model recognizes exceptions to the arguement?
    a. Data
    b. Warrant
    c. Claim
    Δ d. Reservation
    e. Qualifier

16. Which component of the Toumin model provides additional support for the argument's warrant?
    a. Data
    b. Warrant
    c. Reservation
    d. Qualfier
    Δ e. Backing

17. Arguments that contend that something will or will not happen are claims of
    a. fact.
    Δ b. conjecture.
    c. value.
    d. policy.
    e. procedure.

18. Which of the following is NOT a guideline for refutation?
    a. Listen to the argument.
    b. State the claim you oppose.
    c. Overview your objections.
    d. Assemble evidence.
    Δ e. None of the above.

19. Which of the following statements is NOT true?
    a. Men and women approach argument differently.
    b. Men tend to be competitive arguers.
    Δ c. Women tend to view issues as two-sided.
    d. Women tend to seek consensus in a group.
    e. Men and women tend to support arguments with evidence equally.

20. The college is considering a change to the quarter system. Parag opposes it because the college has always been on the semester system. What fallacy is being used?
    a. Ad hominem
    b. Appeal to authority
    Δ c. Appeal to tradition
    d. Faulty analogy
    e. Hasty generalization

True/False

1. Arguing in groups is always disruptive and should be avoided.
   Answer: False

2. An argument is an idea or opinion supported by evidence and reasoning.
   Answer: True

3. Argumentation can improve decision making.
   Answer: True

4. Learning to argue effectively will make you more influential in group decision making.
   Answer: True

5. One of the most significant cultural differences in argumentation is the way people use evidence to support a claim.
   Answer: True

6. Because the interaction is not face-to-face, ad hominem attacks are more acceptable in virtual groups.
   Answer: False

7. Men are more likely than women to use evidence in arguments.
   Answer: False

8. Women tend to search out more different perspectives in argument than do men.
   Answer: True

9. An argument and an opinion are essentially the same concept.
   Answer: False

10. Highly argumentative members dislike having their positions challenged.
    Answer: False

Essay

1. Discuss the values of argument in a group. Using your own experience, provide an example of where such values have been evident.

2. What is the purpose of the Toulmin Model of argument? Draw the model with all of its components. What is the function of each component?

3. Rybacki and Rybacki have identified four ethical responsibilities. Identify and explain the four ethical responsibilities of arguers. What is the importance of each responsibility?

4. What is argumentativeness? Describe the behavior of a highly argumentative group member. How do members' levels of argumentativeness affect the progress of a group toward its goal?

5. Using the steps to refutation discussed in your textbook, explain how you would refute the following claim: "The only way to deal with the increased costs of operating the college is to raise student tuition."

6. The textbook suggests six guidelines for effective refutation. Identify and explain the six guidelines.

7. Discuss the role that gender plays in the argumentative process. Include specific distinctions that you see in male and female argumentation.

8. Discuss the role that culture plays in the argumentative process. Include specific distinctions that you see in the argumentation of people from different cultures.

9. Discuss the impact that cooperative argument can have on groupthink.

10. Discuss the four major steps in presenting an argument. Include both an indication of what those steps are and a specific example of each.

Chapter 11
Motivating Groups

Multiple Choice

1. Which of the following represents an extrinsic reward?
   a. Personal pride in work well done.
   b. The friendship of other group members.
   c. The good opinion of colleagues.
   Δ d. A well-deserved promotion.
   e. Satisfaction of serving others.

2. Expectancy-Value Theory does which of the following?
   a. Explains that punishment and rewards serve different motivational purposes in groups.
   Δ b. Explains why the probability of achieving a goal is as important as the goal itself.
   c. Explains why some women have low achievement needs and fear success.
   d. Explains why group goals should be shared and visionary.
   e. Explains why expectations and values are the same.

3. Which of Maslow's needs would be classified as "satisfiers" rather than "motivators?"
   Δ a. Physiological and safety needs
   b. Safety and belongingness needs
   c. Belongingness and esteem needs
   d. Esteem needs and self-actualization needs
   e. Self-actualization and control needs

4. Which of the following strategies would help motivate group members with strong inclusion needs?
   Δ a. Spend time with them in social settings.
   b. Tell them how valuable they are to the group.
   c. Make them chair of a subcommittee.
   d. Give them special, individual assignments.
   e. Let them know how much you like them as friends.

5. Group members Myers-Briggs® types affect their beliefs about groups. Which of the following beliefs would be characteristic of a perceiver?
   a. Groups can waste time, make decisions too quickly, and create more work.
   b. Groups need to gather and use objective facts but often get bogged down in value and unrealistic discussions.
   c. Groups provide opportunities for cooperation, growth, and friendship.
   d. Groups get work done whey they're structured and task focused.
   Δ e. Groups need freedom to examine possibilities during the discussion process.

6. Kenneth Thomas describes four categories of intrinsic motivation needed to energize and reinforce work. They are

Δ a. inclusion, affection, control, and openness.
b. meaningfulness, choice, competence, and progress.
c. achievement, responsibility, recognition, and advancement.
d. esteem, belongingness, self-actualization, and safety.
e. motivation, assessment, rewards, and punishment.

7. Which of the following questions is not appropriate when trying to decide whether to reprimand a group member?

a. Do you have all the facts concerning the situation?
b. Will the reprimand benefit the group or be counterproductive?
Δ c. Should the group expel the member from the group?
d. Were other group members involved in the incident?
e. Is the group member aware of the rules or standards that have been violated?

8. Which of the following strategies can help you promote a sense of choice within your group?

a. Express enthusiasm; don't be critical or cynical.
b. Set high standards for yourself.
Δ c. Seek and take advantage of new opportunities.
d. Develop a group method for tracking and measuring progress.
e. Recognize and celebrate the accomplishments of others.

9. The textbook suggests four criteria for developing a reward system for groups. Which answer reflects those criteria?

Δ a. Fair; equitable; competitive; appropriate
b. Predictable; immediate; consistent; impersonal
c. Universal; compassionate; standard; final
d. Meaningful; choices of options; based on competencies; progressive
e. Intrinsic; extrinsic; material; personal

10. The textbook suggests four criteria for enacting punishment. Which answer reflects these criteria?

a. Fair; equitable; competitive; appropriate
Δ b. Predictable; immediate; consistent; impersonal
c. Universal; compassionate; standard; final
d. Meaningful; choices of options; based on competencies; progressive
e. Warnings; reprimands; suspension; dismissal

11. Which of the following is NOT a characteristic of individuals with high achievement needs?

a. They take risks when necessary.
b. They are intensely satisfied with success.
Δ c. They are upset with failure even if they tried hard.
d. They select tasks with clear outcomes.
e. They prefer feedback from harsh critics.

12. The most visible symptom of an unmotivated group is
    a. hostility.
Δ b. apathy.
    c. resistance.
    d. non-cooperation.
    e. confusion.

13. Which of the following is NOT an effective tool in motivating virtual groups?
    a. Schedule a face-to-face-meeting.
Δ b. Let the group create its own agenda.
    c. Ensure that everyone contributes.
    d. Structure the meetings with flexibility.
    e. Inject a degree of humor and fun.

14. Which of the following is most true about punishment as a tool?
Δ a. It does not motivate.
    b. It increases productivity.
    c. It increases group cohesiveness.
    d. It increases group commitment.
    e. It should never be used.

15. A reprimand can best be described as
    a. a punishment.
Δ b. a form of feedback that identifies deficiencies.
    c. an action that should only be taken by the leader.
    d. the last step before expulsion.
    e. a personal attack on the member.

16. Which of the following is most true of extrinsic rewards?
Δ a. They are granted by supervisors rather than group members.
    b. They satisfy only physical and safety needs.
    c. They motivate group members to work together.
    d. They appeal to members' passions.
    e. They place primary emphasis on the group's goals.

17. Which of the following is not a type of power?
    a. Reward power
    b. Legitimate power
Δ c. Monetary power
    d. Expert power
    e. Coercive power

18. Which of the following is NOT true of controlling feedback?
    a. It suggests positive outcomes for the group.
    b. It suggests negative outcomes for the group.
    c. It emphasizes the ability to reward.
    d. It emphasizes the ability to punish.
Δ e. Both b and d.

19. A group which limits its membership may be attempting to motivate using which of Maslow's needs?
    a. Physiological needs
    b. Safety needs
Δ c. Esteem needs
    d. Belongingness needs
    e. Self-actualization needs

20. A group may motivate by satisfying which of Schutz's needs?
    a. Need for inclusion
    b. Need for control
    c. Need for affection
    d. Both a and b.
Δ e. All of the above.

True/False

1. Motivation recognizes and financially compensates group members for work well done.
   Answer: False

2. Maslow's belongingness, esteem, and self-actualization needs can be classified as motivators rather than satisfiers.
   Answer: True

3. Men often fear success because they believe it threatens female colleagues.
   Answer: False

4. Meeting self-actualization needs can motivate group members when they provide prestige, status, and a sense of achievement.
   Answer: False

5. Brainstorming works best in a high-inclusion, low-control atmosphere.
   Answer: True

6. In Myers-Briggs® terms, thinkers should be thanked for their analysis but also reminded that logical decisions impact real people.
   Answer: Truc

7. You can motivate judgers by assuring them that they will be given opportunities to reconsider all decisions and make midcourse adjustments whenever needed.
   Answer: False

8. A sense of choice involves motivating members by allowing them to develop a structured plan for achieving their goal.
   Answer: True

9. Reprimands motivate because they threaten to withhold valued extrinsic rewards.
   Answer: False

10. When providing informative feedback, "It" statements focus more on personal traits of individual group members than on the task.
    Answer: False

Essay

1. Explain the differences among motivation, assessment, rewards, and punishment. Use examples to illustrate your understanding of these differences.
2. One writer notes that "You can't buy motivation. It has to come from within." Explain the basis for this conclusion. Use at least two examples to illustrate your point.
3. Choose two of Maslow's five needs and explain how you could motivate group members by satisfying this need. Provide specific examples of the strategies you would use.
4. Choose one of Schultz's interpersonal relationship orientation needs and explain how you could motivate group members by satisfying this need. Provide specific examples of the strategies you would use.
5. Choose two Myers-Briggs® traits and explain how you could motivate group members by adapting to those traits. Provide specific examples of the strategies you would use.
6. Choose two of Kenneth Thompson's four categories of intrinsic motivators needed to energize and reinforce work. Explain how you could motivate group members by enlisting these motivators, Provide specific examples of the strategies you would use.
7. If you decided that a group member should be reprimanded, what guidelines would you follow to make the reprimand effective?
8. If you decided that a group member had to be punished, what guidelines would you follow in enacting the punishment?
9. Describe a situation in which you received an intrinsic and/or extrinsic reward for an action or task you completed. Describe a second situation in which you did not receive any reward for a job well done. Compare your reaction to both situations.
10. Expectancy-Value Theory tries to explain two important components of motivation. What are those components? Explain their function as components of motivation. Provide two examples that demonstrate your understanding of this theory.

Chapter 12
Informed Groups

Multiple Choice

1. A group has decided that each member should summarize his or her research in a brief handout to be distributed to the entire group. Which step of the research process has the group just completed?
   a. The group has just completed assessing present knowledge.
   b. The group has just completed identifying areas needing research.
   c. The group has just completed assigning research responsibilities.
   Δ d. The group has just completed determining how to share the information.
   e. The group has just completed setting deadlines.

2. An article about the extinction of the dinosaurs in *Reader's Digest* refers to research about the late Cretaceous period published in *Scientific American.* The *Scientific American* article would be considered
   a. useless material.
   Δ b. a primary source.
   c. a secondary source.
   d. direct observation.
   e. personal knowledge.

3. A condominium association has appointed a group of residents to decide whether new equipment should be purchased for the fitness center. In order to determine how many people are using the center at specific hours, what would be the best source of information?
   Δ a. Direct observation
   b. Focus groups
   c. Published materials
   d. Electronic databases
   e. Government documents

4. _______________ refers to statements that express an authority's judgement or interpretation.
   a. A fact
   Δ b. Testimony
   c. Statistics
   d. An example
   e. Description

5. Which of the following behaviors should be avoided when using an interview to gather information?
   a. Always scheduling the meeting.
   b. Gather information from other sources first.
   Δ c. Plan to arrive a few minutes late for the interview.
   d. Remind the interviewee of the purpose of the interview.
   e. None of the above.

6. An exploratory research technique that uses a group of carefully selected people to examine a specific research question is referred to as
   a. a primary source.
   b. a secondary source.
Δ c. a focus group.
   d. direct observation.
   e. brainstorming.

7. *The World Almanac* would be considered what type of information source?
   a. Periodical
   b. Government document
   c. Internal document
Δ d. General reference work
   e. Personal knowledge

8. According to a 1993 study by the Families and Work Institute, sixty-five percent of American workers felt that open communication was a very important consideration when selecting the right job. What type of information does this study provide?
   a. Testimony
Δ b. Statistics
   c. Definitions
   d. Descriptions
   e. Examples

9. According to Robert Nelson, a consultant and author of *1,001 Ways to Reward Employees*, managers "should praise publicly and reprimand privately." What type of information does Nelson's advice constitute?
   a. Fact
Δ b. Testimony
   c. Statistics
   d. Examples
   e. Descriptions

10. Which guideline for evaluating evidence asks the following question: "Are these facts and conclusions contrary to the rest of the information the group has collected?"
   a. Source qualification
   b. Recency
   c. Quantity
Δ d. Consistency
   e. Statistical validity

11. Which of the following factors will NOT create a flawed information base for group decision making?
   a. The group rejects useful information.
   b. The group accepts invalid information.
   c. The group gathers too little information.
   d. The group gathers too much information.
Δ e. All of the above.

12. Group members are more likely to share information when
    a. they are not experiencing information overload.
    b. diverse viewpoints exist in the group.
    c. members have specialized expertise.
    d. the group is relatively small.
    Δ e. All of the above.

13. Which of the following is NOT suggested by the textbook as a source of information?
    a. Personal knowledge
    Δ b. Internet chat rooms
    c. Interviews
    d. Focus groups
    e. Electronic data bases

14. Which of the following is true of focus groups?
    a. They are used in the commercial arena.
    b. They are used in politics.
    c. They are difficult to organize
    d. They are difficult to interpret.
    Δ e. All of the above.

15. The policies, procedures, and manuals of an organization are what type of reference material?
    a. General reference works
    b. Periodicals
    c. Government document
    Δ d. Internal documents
    e. Electronic data base

16. Lexis/Nexis is what type of reference material?
    a. General reference work
    b. Periodicals
    c. Government document
    d. Internal document
    Δ e. Electronic data base

17. The Social Science Index is useful for finding information in what type of reference material?
    a. General reference works
    Δ b. Periodicals
    c. Government documents
    d. Internal documents
    e. Books

18. Which of the following can lead to information underload?
    a. Unclear research responsibilities.
    b. The group lacks open communication.
    c. A group lacking cohesiveness.
    d. All of the above.
    Δ e. Both a and b.

19. Which of the following is a legitimate reason to not rely exclusively on books while researching?
    a. They take too long to read.
    b. They contain too much information.
    Δ c. They may contain out-of-date material.
    d. They present only one point of view.
    e. They are written by unqualified sources.

20. The Freedom of Information Act has expanded the availability of what type of reference material?
    a. Books
    b. Periodicals
    Δ c. Government documents
    d. Internal documents
    e. Electronic data bases

True/False

1. According to Hirokawa, "The ability of a group to gather and retain a wide range of information can be the single most important determinant of high-quality decision making."
   Answer: True

2. Group members need only worry about completing their individual research responsibilities. It is not necessary to gather information about the group's overall topic.
   Answer: False

3. The further information is removed from primary sources, the more likely it is that inaccuracies have occurred.
   Answer: True

4. Electronic searches tend to provide outdated information compared to most other sources of information.
   Answer: False

5. The way in which a source chooses to report a statistic can conceal or distort the information.
   Answer: True

6. The most reliable source of information is the Internet.
   Answer: False

7. The amount and accuracy of information is a critical factor in predicting a group's success.
   Answer: True

8. Most group members do a good job of keeping one another informed.
   Answer: False

9. Deadlines for group information gathering should be very flexible.
   Answer: False

10. Primary sources are always superior to secondary sources.
    Answer: False

Essay

1. Assume you have arranged an interview with a well-informed expert on your group's topic. Describe the guidelines you will follow when you conduct the interview.

2. The authors of your textbook suggest that during an initial meeting a group should discuss how it is going to become better informed. What steps should a group follow to accomplish this objective? What is the importance of each step?

3. Hirokawa and Scheerhorn claim that errors that occur in a group's information base "are likely to contribute to faulty decision making." What factors can create a flawed information base? What are the potential effects of a flawed information base on group decision making?

4. Your textbook presents general questions a group should ask when evaluating information. Identify and explain each of those questions.

5. Discuss the concept of focus groups. Include in your answer an indication of what they are, when they may be used and the difficulties of using them.

6. Describe the problems that arise from relying solely on the internet for all the research on a given topic.

7. The textbook identifies six common types of information. Identify and define each of the six types.

8. Discuss the major problems that exist in a group that may result in a flawed information base.

9. Statistics are often regarded as totally objective. Discuss some of the factors that should be considered before accepting the statistics.

10. Discuss the impact that both information underload and information overload have on the group communication process. Include in your answer an indication of why such problems arise.

Chapter 13
Technology and Virtual Groups

Multiple Choice

1. For an electronic meeting you should determine
   a. why you are meeting.
   b. where you should meet.
   c. what materials you will need before or during the meeting.
   d. Both a and b.
Δ e. All of the above.

2. Which of the following items is NOT listed in the textbook as a technique for making conference calls more successful?
   a. Prepare and follow an agenda.
   b. Adapt to the oral only channel.
Δ c. Do vocal warm ups before the call.
   d. Introduce yourself before talking.
   e. All of the above.

3. In a computer conference, <g> is an example of
Δ a. an emoticon.
   b. asynchronous communication.
   c. a happicon.
   d. a symbolic reference.
   e. punctuation.

4. Your textbook divides computer conferences into the following two categories
   a. typical and atypical.
   b. serial and parallel.
   c. online and off-line.
Δ d. synchronous and asynchronous.
   e. modem and network.

5. Which of the following consequences is a drawback of teleconferencing?
   a. Group members may feel isolated.
   b. Group members may work on other tasks during a conference call.
   c. Group cohesion may be reduced.
Δ d. All of the above.
   e. None of the above.

6. E-mail is an example of
   a. parallel communication.
   b. serial communication.
   c. synchronous communication.
Δ d. asynchronous communication.
   e. All of the above.

7. Computer conferences that occur simultaneously in real-time are examples of
   a. parallel communication.
   b. serial communication.
   Δ c. synchronous communication.
   d. asynchronous communication.
   e. All of the above.

8. According to the textbook, typing a message in a computer conference using all capital letters
   a. is faster.
   b. makes it easier to read.
   Δ c. may be interpreted as anger.
   d. All of the above.
   e. None of the above.

9. According to the authors of your textbook, software and hardware that provide group members with the ability to generate and evaluate ideas, make decisions, and use different voting procedures is known as
   a. meetingware.
   Δ b. group support systems.
   c. decisionware.
   d. taskware.
   e. problemware.

10. A _______________ is a coordinated phone call among three or more group members.
    a. videoconference
    Δ b. teleconference
    c. group support system
    d. meetingware session
    e. computerized meeting

11. A virtual place for meeting is referred to as
    a. computerized meetings.
    b. cybermeeting.
    Δ c. cyberspace.
    d. asynchronous.
    e. synchronous.

12. Which of the following is NOT an advantage of teleconferences over other forms of electronic meetings?
    Δ a. Members are less likely to work on nongroup work during the meeting.
    b. It is easy to set up and use.
    c. It requires the least investment in equipment.
    d. Both a and c.
    e. All of the above.

13. Which of the following is an advantage of synchronous communication?
    a. There is more time to compose responses.
    b. Document review and editing is facilitated.
    Δ c. There is more spontaneous and dynamic interaction.
    d. All of the above.
    e. None of the above.

14. Major corporations such as Boeing and IBM report that computer software has cut meeting time by approximately
    a. 10 %.
    b. 25 %.
    Δ c. 50 %.
    d. 75 %.
    e. 90 %.

15. At the conclusion of an audio conference, which of the following is NOT considered important?
    a. Summarize the discussion.
    b. Describe the next step.
    c. Set a date and time for the next meeting.
    d. Distribute the minutes as soon as possible.
    Δ e. None of the above.

16. Which of the following is NOT true of audio conferences?
    a. They are easy to set up and use.
    b. They are effective ways to solve problems.
    Δ c. They are effective in negotiating interpersonal conflicts.
    d. They may be the best method for resolving emergencies.
    e. The quantity and quality of participation may decrease.

17. Which of the following is a characteristic of asynchronous communication?
    a. It is linear.
    b. Immediate feedback is not received.
    c. It is not interactive.
    d. It is more deliberate than synchronous communication.
    Δ e. All of the above.

18. Which of the following is NOT considered a type of groupware?
    a. Email
    b. Bulletin boards
    c. Electronic chat
    d. Electronic meeting systems
    Δ e. Videoconferencing

19. Which of the following is NOT an advantage of using Email?
    a. It is asynchronous.
    b. It allows time for reflection.
  Δ c. It reduces nonverbal influences.
    d. It produces a written record.
    e. It allows for quick dissemination of information.

20. Which of the following is NOT an advantage of electronic meeting systems?
    a. It is good for brainstorming.
  Δ b. It requires little technical training and assistance.
    c. It facilitates collaboration.
    d. It involves anonymity.
    e. It inhibits groupthink.

True/False

1. It is a good idea to prepare an agenda for a teleconference.
   Answer: True

2. The preparation for a videoconference is the same as it would be for a face-to-face meeting.
   Answer: False

3. Emoticons are substitutes for nonverbal messages in text-only communication.
   Answer: True

4. You should try to dazzle your audience with multimedia effects during a presentation.
   Answer: False

5. Technology has become an inevitable component of groupwork.
   Answer: True

6. Teleconferences are more complicated to set up than videoconferences.
   Answer: False

7. When group members use computers to interact simultaneously in real time, they are engaged in synchronous communication.
   Answer: Truc

8. Virtual groups always communicate asynchronously.
   Answer: False

9. Videoconferencing is the fastest type of communication used by virtual groups.
   Answer: False

10. Electronic chat environments may lead to difficulties in verifying information.
    Answer: True

Essay

1. Identify the differences between synchronous and asynchronous communication and discuss the advantages and disadvantages of their usage.

2. What is a teleconference? What is a videoconference? What is a computer conference? What are the pros and cons of using each type of electronic meeting?

3. The authors of your textbook maintain that new technologies provide tools, not toys. What is the difference? How does a group decide when the use of technology should be used?

4. Discuss the process of participating in a videoconference. Include in your answer an indication of the tools that can be used to make videoconferencing easier to conduct.

5. Discuss the process of participating in an audioconference. Include in your answer an indication of the tools that can be used to make audioconferencing easier to conduct.

6. Discuss the advantages and disadvantages of conducting meetings through audioconferencing.

7. Discuss the advantages and disadvantages of conducting meetings through videoconferencing.

8. Discuss the advantages and disadvantages of both synchronous and asynchronous communication.

9. Discuss the process of participating in text-based computer communication. Include in your answer an indication of the tools that can be used to make text-based computer communication easier to use.

10. Discuss the advantages and disadvantages of conducting meetings through text-based computer communication.

Chapter 14
Planning and Conducting Meetings

Multiple Choice

1. Which of the following reasons is sound justification for scheduling or attending a meeting?
   a. You hate to write reports and memos.
   b. You prefer not to do the research yourself.
   c. You feel lost without colleagues.
   Δ d. Group input and interaction is critical.
   e. All of the above.

2. One hundred or more people gathered to listen to a speaker deliver a presentation is
   a. a small group meeting.
   Δ b. an assembly.
   c. a council.
   d. a governance group.
   e. an *ad hoc* committee.

3. A meeting of 40 or 50 people in which the group listens to several speakers with some audience participation is
   a. a small group meeting.
   b. an assembly.
   Δ c. a council.
   d. a governance group.
   e. an *ad hoc* committee.

4. Which of the following items is NOT the responsibility of a meeting's chairperson?
   a. Notify everyone who should attend.
   b. Prepare for participation in the discussion.
   c. Distribute minutes and reports after the meeting.
   d. Keep the group focused on the task.
   Δ e. All of the above.

5. According to the textbook, which of the following elements best defines a group meeting?
   a. Schedule; agenda; structure
   b. Size; frequency; setting
   c. Structure; setting; chairperson
   Δ d. Schedule; structure; chairperson
   e. Size; agenda; structure

6. The person appointed or elected to conduct a meeting is the
   a. group leader.
   b. dominator.
   Δ c. chairperson.
   d. nonparticipant.
   e. recorder.

7. When determining who should be invited to a meeting, which of the following criteria should NOT be included as a consideration?
   a. Individuals who will be affected directly by the outcome.
   b. Individuals with special expertise.
   c. Individuals who disagree or represent minority viewpoints.
   d. Individuals who have the power to implement decisions.
Δ e. Individuals who are unaware or uninvolved in the issues scheduled for discussion.

8. When members are late to a meeting, the chairperson should
   a. wait to start until all members have arrived.
   b. review what has been accomplished whenever a latecomer arrives.
Δ c. let latecomers sit without participating until they have observed enough to be able to contribute.
   d. publicly reprimand latecomers.
   e. assign latecomers tasks that no one else wants to do.

9. Which of the following labels does NOT represent a "people problem" in groups?
   a. Loudmouth
   b. Interrupter
   c. Whisperer
   d. Latecomer
Δ e. Tension releaser

10. What does your textbook suggest a group can do to deal with a loudmouth?
   a. Interrupt
   b. Have that person take minutes.
   c. Acknowledge that person's ideas.
   d. Ask for viewpoints from other members.
Δ e. All of the above.

11. According to Dodd, group members in which of the following countries expect more directive leadership and control.
Δ a. Mexico
   b. Denmark
   c. Australia
   d. Israel
   e. United States

13. _______________ is the outline of items to be discussed and the tasks to be accomplished at a meeting.
   a. A set of minutes
   b. An action item
Δ c. An agenda
   d. A report
   e. A call to order

14. At what point in the agenda does a chairperson officially begin a meeting?
Δ a. The call to order.
   b. During the approval of the agenda.
   c. During the approval of the previous meeting's minutes.
   d. After reports from individuals and subcommittees.
   e. After unfinished business is completed.

15. The Committee to Save the Park began a discussion of plans to organize a park clean-up day. There was not enough time during the meeting to finish the discussion. In what part of the agenda for the next meeting should this issue appear?
   a. Call to order
   b. Reports from individuals and subcommittees
Δ c. Unfinished business
   d. New business
   e. Announcements

16. According to the guidelines presented in the textbook, when is the best time to address important and difficult issues?
   a. At the beginning of the meeting.
Δ b. During the middle portion of the meeting.
   c. During the last third of the meeting.
   d. At the end of the meeting.
   e. These items do not need to be placed on the agenda.

17. The elections committee of the Student Government Council is making preparations for the upcoming campus elections. During what part of the agenda should the elections committee chairperson report on the status of the committee's work?
   a. Call to order
   b. Unfinished business
   c. New business
   d. Announcements
Δ e. Reports from individuals and subcommittees

18. The written record of a group's discussion and activities is referred to as
Δ a. the minutes.
   b. an action itcm.
   c. an agenda.
   d. a report.
   e. a call to order.

19. Which of the following statements about the minutes of a meeting is NOT true?
   a. The format of the minutes should follow the format of the agenda.
   b. The more formal the meeting the more information must be included in the minutes.
   c. The minutes must be accurate and impartial.
Δ d. The minutes are a word-for-word record of everything that members say.
   e. The chairperson should delegate the task of taking minutes to another member.

20. How far in advance of a meeting does the textbook suggest distributing the agenda?
    - a. One hour
    - b. One day
    - c. Two days
    - Δ d. One week
    - e. One month

True/False

1. If there is nothing important to talk about, a meeting can do more harm than good.
   Answer: True
2. A coincidental gathering of group members does not constitute a meeting.
   Answer: True
3. The purpose of a meeting is the same as the topic of discussion.
   Answer: False
4. The chairperson of a meeting is always the group's leader.
   Answer: False
5. A chairperson's job is complete when a meeting adjourns.
   Answer: False
6. A face-to face group meeting is better than communicating via a memo, fax, email, or voice mail.
   Answer: False
7. By looking through a group's minutes over a period of time, you can determine how productive the group has been.
   Answer: True
8. Minutes can never be considered legal documents.
   Answer: False
9. Once the chairperson has prepared an agenda, group members should not request modifications or additions before or during the meeting.
   Answer: False
10. All meetings follow the traditional sequence of agenda items.
    Answer: False

Essay

1. The success or failure of a meeting largely depends on proper planning. According to the textbook, what five questions should you ask yourself as you plan a meeting? Why is each one important? What are the potential consequences of ignoring any one of the questions?
2. What should an effective chairperson do prior to a meeting? What is the chairperson's role during a meeting? After a meeting is over, what should the chairperson do?

3. Why should all group members arrive on time and stay for the duration of a meeting? What can a chairperson or other group member do to discourage members from arriving late or leaving early?
4. What is the purpose of an agenda for a meeting? Why is an agenda important?
5. What items will a traditional business meeting agenda include? Demonstrate your ability to prepare an agenda by outlining the agenda for a hypothetical group meeting.
6. Why is it important to record the minutes of a meeting? Who is responsible for the minutes? What are the guidelines for well-done minutes?
7. In setting up a virtual meeting, a planner should follow several different guidelines. Identify and explain those guidelines.
8. Often, meetings are regarded as a waste of time. Identify and discuss five reasons why this perception may exist.
9. Disruptive individuals may undermine a meeting. Identify five of the typical behaviors that may pose problems for a group meeting.
10. Discuss the process for evaluating a meeting.

Chapter 15
Making Presentations in Groups

Multiple Choice

1. The first and most important guideline for an oral presentation is determining your purpose. Purpose raises which question?
   a. Is there a natural order to the ideas and information you want to include in your presentation?
Δ b. What do you want listeners to know, think, believe, or do as a result of your presentation?
   c. How can you use information about your listeners to improve your presentation?
   d. Where and how can you find good ideas and information for your presentation?
   e. How can you adapt to the place where you will be speaking?

2. Which of the following items would be considered when analyzing the demographic traits of an audience or group of listeners?
Δ a. Gender
   b. Job titles
   c. Special interests
   d. Relationships with other members
   e. Length of group membership

3. Which of the following items would be considered when analyzing the individual attributes of audience members for an oral presentation?
   a. Gender
Δ b. Job titles
   c. Race
   d. Religion
   e. Ethnicity

4. When you identify a belief or value that you share with audience members who disagree, you have found a basis for
   a. demographic traits.
   b. individual attributes.
   c. claim of value.
Δ d. common ground.
   e. personal credibility.

5. What is the size and shape of the room? Do I need a microphone? Will I make the presentation in the morning or afternoon? What is my time limit? Which oral presentation guideline is addressed by these questions?
Δ a. Place
   b. Preparation
   c. Planning
   d. Performance
   e. Purpose

6. What organizational pattern would be most effective for an oral presentation designed to explain a company's hiring procedures, step-by-step?
   Δ a. Time arrangement
   b. Space arrangement
   c. Problem-solution
   d. Comparison-contrast
   e. Causes and effects

7. An outline for an oral presentation should include
   a. the central idea.
   b. the main points of the speech.
   c. indications of supporting material.
   d. an introduction and conclusion.
   Δ e. All of the above.

8. If listeners conclude at the end of an oral presentation that you lack expertise on the subject and question your honesty and sincerity, you have failed to devote enough attention to
   a. people.
   b. place.
   c. planning.
   d. performance.
   Δ e. personal credibility.

9. Which of the following is NOT listed in your textbook as a guideline when preparing computer-based presentation aids?
   a. Exercise restraint.
   Δ b. Use at least three fonts.
   c. Choose a modest background.
   d. Don't overuse multimedia effects.
   e. Choose readable typefaces.

10. Which of the following behaviors should you avoid when using visual aids as part of an oral presentation?
    a. Explain the visual aid to the listeners.
    b. Give listeners enough time to look at the visual aid.
    Δ c. Face the visual aid, not your listeners, when speaking.
    d. Be prepared to give your presentation without your visual aids.
    e. You should do all of the above when using visual aids.

11. The textbook identifies two major factors that enhance a speaker's credibility. What are they?
    Δ a. Competence and character
    b. Attitude and appearance
    c. Demographics and individual attributes
    d. Common ground and competence
    e. Purpose and place

12. An oral presentation discussing why recycling is needed and how the community can implement a more effective program is probably using which organizational pattern?
    a. Time arrangement
    b. Space arrangement
    Δ c. Problem-solution
    d. Comparison-contrast
    e. Causes and effects

13. Which of the following is NOT a guideline suggested by your textbook for handling a question-and-answer session?
    a. Don't change the subject.
    b. Be specific.
    Δ c. Provide the most comprehensive answer possible.
    d. Be honest. If you don't know the answer, admit it.
    e. Be brief.

14. Which of the following is NOT considered a demographic trait?
    a. Age
    b. Gender
    c. Race
    Δ d. Knowledge level
    e. Religion

15. If an audience disagrees with your position before your presentation begins, which of the following are effective strategies?
    a. Set realistic goals.
    b. Find common ground.
    c. Support your arguments with evidence.
    d. Both b and c.
    Δ e. All of the above.

16. Which of the following are the major factors contributing to credibility?
    a. Competence and appearance
    b. Character and appearance
    c. Appearance and organization
    Δ d. Competence and character
    e. Character and organization

17. Which of the following should NOT be done with presentational software?
    a. Make only one point per slide.
    b. Follow the 6x6 rule.
    Δ c. Use multiple typefaces.
    d. Use consistent backgrounds.
    e. Resist the overuse of clipart.

18. What organizational pattern would be most effective for an oral presentation assessing the merits of two possible proposals?
    a. Time arrangement
    b. Space arrangement
    c. Problem-solution
    Δ d. Compare and contrast
    e. Cause and effect

19. What organizational pattern would be most effective for an oral presentation calling for changes in the national system for homeland security?
    a. Time arrangement
    b. Space arrangement
    Δ c. Problem-solution
    d. Compare and contrast
    e. Cause and effect

20. Which of the following is the single most important delivery characteristic for an effective oral presentation?
    Δ a. Eye contact
    b. Articulation
    c. Volume
    d. Pitch
    e. Pronunciation

True/False

1. The reputation and quality of a group may be judged by how well members succeed as speakers.
   Answer: True

2. Having a clear purpose ensures that it will be achieved during an oral presentation.
   Answer: False

3. When preparing your oral presentation, you should collect a lot of information and try to use it all.
   Answer: False

4. Impromptu speaking is a form of delivery without advance preparation or practice.
   Answer: True

5. A team presentation is simply a collection of individual speeches, one right after the other.
   Answer: False

6. Demographic traits include age, gender, race, ethnicity, religion, and marital status.
   Answer: True

7. Audience adaptation is the most important guideline in developing an oral presentation.
   Answer: False

8. Purpose and topic refer to the same concept in oral presentations.
   Answer: False

9. The body of an oral presentation should always contain three major points.
Answer: False

10. The use of presentational software always enhances the communicative message.
Answer: False

Essay

1. The textbook recommends that a speaker follow seven critical decision-making guidelines when preparing an oral presentation. What are the seven questions a group member should consider when preparing a presentation? Explain the importance of each guideline.

2. What is meant by personal credibility? Who determines whether you are seen as a credible speaker? Identify and explain the significance of two factors that are particularly important in determining a speaker's credibility.

3. What is the difference between an oral presentation's purpose and its topic? Demonstrate your understanding of the difference by providing an example of a purpose and a topic for a hypothetical presentation.

4. What is a team presentation? In what ways is a team presentation similar to or different than a speech presented by a single, independent speaker?

5. Discuss several of the guidelines that should be considered when making a presentation in a virtual group. Provide specific examples to illustrate your points.

6. Identify and explain five organizational patterns for developing an oral presentation. Include in your answer an indication of the types of presentations each is best suited for.

7. Discuss the major guidelines for the use of presentation aids in an oral presentation. Include in your discussion several types of such aids.

8. Discuss five major guidelines for the use of presentation software in an oral presentation.

9. Some presentations include a Question-and-Answer session. Discuss three guidelines a speaker should follow in responding to questions.

10. Discuss the major guidelines for effective vocal and physical delivery in an oral presentation. Include in your answer an indication of how each can be improved.

Appendix
Parliamentary Procedure

Multiple Choice

1. The earliest example of parliamentary procedure can be found in
   Δ a. the British Parliament.
   b. the U.S. Senate.
   c. the U.S. House of Representatives.
   d. Thomas Jefferson's writings.
   e. Henry M. Robert's rules.

2. Parliamentary procedure should be used when
   a. a group wants to ensure that everyone has an opportunity to speak.
   b. a group has a limited amount of time.
   c. a group's decision has legal implications.
   d. a group wants all points of view to be shared.
   Δ e. parliamentary procedure should be used for all of the above reasons.

3. The rules governing how an organization operates are often included in the organization's constitution or
   a. parliamentary procedure.
   b. quorum.
   c. motion.
   Δ d. bylaws.
   e. agenda.

4. Which of the following statements is NOT true of parliamentary procedure?
   a. Only one person may speak at a time.
   Δ b. Several subjects may be discussed at the same time.
   c. The chairperson is primarily responsible for ensuring that the rules are followed.
   d. The group may not make a decision unless the meeting is properly called.
   e. All of the above.

5. _______________ is a systematic method used by groups to determine the majority's will.
   a. A bylaw
   b. Brainstorming
   c. E-mail
   d. The Standard Agenda
   Δ e. Parliamentary procedure

6. The minimum number or percentage of voting members who must be present at a meeting in order to transact business is referred to as a
   a. majority.
   b. precedence.
   c. second.
   d. floor.
   Δ e. quorum.

7. Who is ultimately responsible for making sure that the rules of parliamentary procedure are enforced?
   a. Sergeant at arms
   b. Secretary
   Δ c. Chair
   d. Parliamentarian
   e. Clerk

8. In a group using parliamentary procedure, who is responsible for taking the minutes and providing a record of the results of all votes?
   a. Sergeant at arms
   b. Presiding officer
   c. Chair
   d. Parliamentarian
   Δ e. Clerk

9. How should a motion be introduced?
   a. "I motion that. . ."
   b. "We should put in motion. . ."
   c. "I suggest a movement to. . ."
   Δ d. "I move that. . ."
   e. "I propose the following movement."

10. A relatively large group using parliamentary procedure is having difficulty seeing and hearing when members speak. A member wants to suggest that speakers stand up and speak louder. What type of motion should the member make?
   a. Call for the orders of the day.
   b. Move the previous question.
   c. Limit or extend debate.
   d. Point of order.
   Δ e. Question of privilege.

11. If a member wants to suggest that the group end debate on an issue and vote immediately, what type of motion should be made?
   a. Call for the orders of the day.
   Δ b. Move the previous question.
   c. Limit or extend debate.
   d. Point of order.
   e. Question of privilege.

12. When a member wants the group to vote on an issue, what is the most appropriate way to make such a request?
    a. "I move the previous question."
    Δ b. "I make a movement that we vote."
    c. "Who wants to vote?"
    d. "I question the vote."
    e. "I move that we table the motion."

13. Parliamentary procedure may be dispensed with under what conditions?
    a. When a group is large.
    Δ b. When a group faces little controversy.
    c. When a group has limited time.
    d. When a group is formal.
    e. It may never be dispensed with.

14. Which of the following is a rationale for the use of parliamentary procedure?
    a. Equal opportunity for all members.
    b. Balanced discussion.
    c. Protection of minority rights.
    d. Both a and b.
    Δ e. All of the above.

15. Which of the following motions may NOT be amended?
    a. To limit or extend debate.
    b. To postpone indefinitely.
    c. To refer to committee.
    Δ d. To recess.
    e. To amend the amendment.

16. Which of the following motions requires a 2/3 approval?
    a. Adjourn
    b. Table
    Δ c. Limit/extend debate
    d. Postpone indefinitely
    e. Recess

17. Which motion allows one to interrupt the speaker?
    a. Amendment
    Δ b. Question of privilege
    c. Previous question
    d. Postpone indefinitely
    e. Recess

18. Which of the following may NOT be debated?
    a. Main motion
    b. Amendment
    Δ c. Point of order
    d. Refer to committee
    e. Postpone indefinitely

19. Under parliamentary procedure, who may participate and vote?
    a. All those in attendance.
    Δ b. Only official group members.
    c. Only members with perfect attendance.
    d. All those the groups approves as voters.
    e. All except the chair.

20. Which of the following is true of parliamentarians?
    a. They must be appointed in every group.
    b. They must be a member of the group.
    Δ c. They must have a thorough knowledge of parliamentary procedure.
    d. They have the final say on parliamentary issues.
    e. All of the above.

True/False

1. All meetings should use parliamentary procedure.
   Answer: False

2. Parliamentary procedure is based upon the principle of majority rule.
   Answer: True

3. A person who seconds a motion must vote for the motion.
   Answer: False

4. A second is not required in order for a main motion to be discussed.
   Answer: False

5. In less formal groups, the chair is usually permitted to join the discussion and make motions.
   Answer: True

6. In order for parliamentary procedure to be useful, a group must strictly adhere to all of the rules.
   Answer: False

7. Parliamentary procedure is widely used but not well understood by its users.
   Answer: True

8. Most group members use parliamentary procedures to achieve some ulterior goal.
   Answer: False

9. All members share the responsibility of ensuring that parliamentary rules are followed.
   Answer: True

10. In informal groups, issues may be discussed at great length before a specific motion is made.
    Answer: True

Essay

1. What is parliamentary procedure? What purpose does it serve for groups? When should a group use parliamentary procedure?
2. The textbook discusses five basic principles of parliamentary procedure. Identify and explain each principle. How does parliamentary procedure help accomplish each principle?
3. Making a motion involves six steps. Identify and explain each step. Demonstrate your ability to use parliamentary procedure by describing each step in a hypothetical motion.
4. What is a privileged request? What are the major types of privileged requests? Under what circumstances might a member make privileged requests?
5. Discuss the roles and responsibilities of a chair operating under parliamentary procedure. Include in your answer an indication of what the chair may and may not do in a meeting.
6. Discuss some of the differences in using parliamentary procedure in formal and informal groups. Use specific examples to illustrate your point.
7. Discuss some of the ways that parliamentary procedure may be used in a negative manner. Include in your answer ways of avoiding such problems.
8. Compare and contrast the concepts of majority rule and minority rights in parliamentary procedure. Include in your discussion specific procedures designed to protect each.
9. Discuss the concept of a quorum. Include in your answer both an indication of what it is and why it is used in parliamentary procedure.
10. Discuss the role of a parliamentarian in formal meetings. Include in your answer an indication of what characteristics are necessary in a parliamentarian, what the duties are and what the powers are.